ECHOES
THROUGH TIME

By

William K. Mackie

ISBN: 978-1-09727-250-1

Dedicated to the Memory of

Margaret Christina **"Peggy"** Dunlop
1926 -2020

Her smile and her infectious laughter will be sadly missed

Preface

The Scottish War Blinded – the beginning

Scottish National Institution for Blinded Soldiers and Sailors

At a meeting in January 1915, the committee running the Scottish National Institution for the Blind discussed the duty devolving upon them to do something to meet the needs of Scottish soldiers and sailors who had lost or might lose their sight in the War, and the facilities for instruction in Braille which they had at West Craigmillar, Edinburgh.

It was remitted to the Chairman and Committee members to obtain particulars of Scottish soldiers and sailors blinded in the War, and to report what action the Institution should take to meet their needs in the way of blind instruction and training.

On Wednesday, 14 April 1915, at a meeting at 58 Nicolson Street, the Chairman reported that it had come to his knowledge that the National Institute for the Blind in London had appointed a collector in Edinburgh.

As a result, he had inserted an advertisement in The Scotsman, calling attention to the fact that the Scottish Institution was organizing a scheme to deal with blinded sailors and soldiers, and asking the public meantime to withhold support from the National Institute's appeal.

He had also written a letter to the Editor of The Scotsman to the same effect. It was noted that enquiries had been made at the Scottish Military Headquarters about the numbers of blinded soldiers, and a letter from Reverend Dr Patrick R Mackay, Chaplain to the Forces, indicated that the military authorities were to furnish the Institution with full particulars of all soldiers whose vision had suffered through the war.

The Committee recommended that the Institution establish in Edinburgh a training centre where blind Scottish sailors and soldiers could be "taught to be blind", to trained to read and write in Braille and trained in suitable handicrafts. If necessary, a residence or hostel was to be established for the temporary accommodation of those receiving training.

The Scottish Branch of the British Red Cross Society, the various Scottish Institutions and Societies for the Blind, and the Naval and Military Authorities, were invited to co-operate in the work by reporting to the Institution all blind sailors and soldiers coming to their attention.

Application was made to the National Relief (Prince of Wales) Fund, and the Scottish Red Cross Society, for grants to meet the expenses to be incurred, and an appeal was made to the public for subscriptions.

On Thursday, 1st July a concert was held in the Central Hall for the benefit of the Scottish Women's Hospital for work in Serbia, and the Institution's Annual Sale of Work was held at West Craigmillar on Friday, 2 July.

The concert in Central Hall raised £40 9s 9d after deductions for expenses. The total sum handed to the Scottish Women's Hospital for work in Serbia became £45 when £1 10s 3d was added from the entertainment put on by children in the Institution's gymnasium, and a sum of £3 voted for school prizes which was given by children.

At this time the Institution was hoping to be recognised by the War Department as the training centre in Scotland for blinded soldiers and sailors. This appeal was launched in 1915.

On Thursday, 27 January 1916, approval was given by the Board for an application to the War Office for recognition of the Institution as the Scottish Training Centre for Blinded Soldiers and Sailors, and to take all steps necessary to follow up the application and to secure the recognition desired.

The Lord Advocate had agreed to receive a deputation from the Directors on the matter, the Lord Provost was taking an interest, and had offered to countersign the application as having his cordial support.

It was agreed that a deputation would go to London if thought advisable.

At a meeting at 58 Nicolson Street on Tuesday, 22 February 1916, it was recorded that the Lord Advocate had received a deputation favourably and promised to write the Secretary for Scotland and the Under-Secretary of State for War in support of the Asylum's application.

Members of Parliament for the City and for Leith Burghs had been approached to support the application.

At a meeting at 58 Nicolson Street on Friday, 25 February 1916, it was reported that Newington House, which contained 21 rooms, and had extensive grounds and ample offices, might be secured, and an offer had been made to lease the house for five years from Whitsunday 1916, with a mutual break at the end of three years, at a rent of £200 per annum. It was understood the offer would be accepted.

In view of this it was resolved not to renew the tenancy of the hostel at 37 Grange Loan and to transfer the music students to Newington House. The arrangements made by the Asylum were communicated to the War Department. The Asylum's offer to lease Newington House was accepted and a letter was sent to the present tenants, Dr and Mrs Bartholomew, thanking them for the way they had helped the Institution in the matter.

Newington House was built by the distinguished Edinburgh surgeon, Benjamin Bell of Hunthill, in 1805. Many prominent people lived in the area, for example, Andrew Usher, the Edinburgh Brewer and donor of the Usher Hall. Some of the villas in the area also housed the famous - David Octavius Hill, the pioneer photographer, who helped found the Royal Scottish Academy, lived in Newington Lodge, on the corner of Mayfield Terrace and Dalkeith Road.

Dr Joseph Bell, the inspiring teacher of Arthur Conan Doyle and, allegedly, an early model for Sherlock Holmes, was the first resident of 44 Blacket Place. Newington House on Blacket Avenue was occupied by Dr John Bartholomew of the famous map-making firm, whose Edinburgh Geological Institute was opened in nearby Duncan Street in 1911. From 1915 Newington House became the centre for the Scottish National Institute for the War Blinded but eventually fell into disrepair and was demolished in the 1960s. The site was then purchased by the University of Edinburgh, which built student flats there.

A public meeting in support of the Institution's scheme for dealing with Blinded Scottish Soldiers and Sailors was arranged to be held in the Council Chambers on Tuesday, 7 March, at 3 pm, under the chairmanship of the Lord Provost.

In May 1916 a deputation went to London and had meetings with the Scottish Members of Parliament, the Lord Advocate, and the Secretary for Scotland, and afterwards had an interview with the Under-Secretary of State for War and the Secretary of the Army Council. The Asylum deputation had been sympathetically received in all quarters, and it was expected that recognition would be granted. In July 1916, the death was recorded of the Institution's physician, Dr Melville Dunlop.

For 27 years he had enjoyed the full confidence of the Directors for the way he fulfilled his duties towards the workers, by whom he was trusted. In 1915 his services were required by the military authorities for work among the soldiers at the Front, and the Directors had granted him leave of absence, which, because of his services at a Base Hospital in France, had to be extended on two occasions. His health was undermined as a result of his devotion to duty.

In October 1916, a letter was received from Lord Derby recognising Newington House as the Scottish National Institution for training blinded soldiers. Scottish military hospitals were now advising the superintendent of Newington House of all blinded men entering these hospitals. A special paid representative of Newington House was appointed in London, with full powers to make all arrangements necessary to secure the transfer of blinded men from London to Newington House.

The Directors are happy to report that this scheme has been successfully launched. A very generous response has been made to their appeal to the Scottish public to provide in Scotland for Scotsmen blinded in the war. Newington House, to which entry was obtained at Whitsunday, is admirably adapted as a residence and training centre for the men. It is comfortable and commodious and the grounds by which it is surrounded are exceedingly beautiful.

The principal Outdoor Teaching Societies have been invited to co-operate in carrying out the scheme, and representatives of the Edinburgh Society for Teaching the Blind to Read, the Fife and Kinross Society for Teaching the Blind, and the Aberdeen Association for Teaching the Blind have joined the Committee. Sir Robert K Inches has also become a Member of Committee, and the Directors take this opportunity of acknowledging the invaluable services which, as Lord Provost of the City, he has rendered to the furthering of the scheme.

It is gratifying also to record that the War Office has recognised Newington House as the Scottish National Centre for the training and instruction of blinded soldiers and sailors.

Quite a number of men have already been benefitted by the scheme. There has, however, been some little unavoidable delay in completing the arrangements for getting in touch with the men at No 2 General Hospital, Chelsea, where men whose sight has been destroyed or injured are, as far as possible, sent. The Scottish Command has also arranged for Newington House to be advised of all blinded men in Scottish military hospitals. It is expected, therefore, that the accommodation at Newington House will be fully utilized shortly.

While the instruction and training which the blinded men will receive immediately after reception loom largest in the public eye meantime - and perhaps also in the minds of the men themselves - the Directors would emphasise that such instruction and training are but the beginning of the work. The aftercare of the men will be the real burden.

When the training is completed there will remain a long, long vista of years - for all our soldiers are young men - during which they will have to be provided with work, cared for and cheered. And the glamour of wartime will then be over, the enthusiasm for war charities will have vanished; but the men will remain, the sightless eyes will remain, and the need will probably be as great 10 years, 15 years hence, as today. Nay, perhaps greater as Scotsmen trained elsewhere will in later years gravitate back to Scotland.

It is for this later and permanent burden, as well as the present need, that the Newington House scheme is intended to provide. The Directors would very earnestly urge that it is of the utmost importance that a Large Permanent Fund should be provided now, so that in days to come, when public interest is elsewhere, Scotland's blinded sons may rest secure without fear of pinch or poverty.

The Newington House Fund is of course kept entirely separate and administered apart, from the General Funds of The Royal Bind Asylum and School. A 1916 Report on Newington House One of the most interesting developments of the work of the Royal Blind Asylum during the past year had been the effort made to assist sailors and soldiers blinded in the war.

The exigencies of transport and the necessity for finding accommodation for casualties from the battlefield have resulted in the distribution of wounded men throughout the hospitals of this country, in the first instance, without regard to their nationality, domicile, or proper military headquarters. Thus, the majority of Scotsmen suffering from injury to their eyes and eyesight have been treated in English hospitals, while many Englishmen have at first been committed to the care of Scottish surgeons.

Although at a later stage those who are sufficiently recovered to return to duty have been gradually drafted back to their own regimental depots, the more seriously damaged, when discharged as unfit for further service, may still be far from home.

Under these circumstances, several Scottish soldiers blinded in the earlier stages of the war have found their way to the institution organised at St Dunstan's, Regent's Park, London, by Sir Arthur Pearson. The Directors of the Blind Asylum are well aware of the difficulty which we have had in Edinburgh of getting into communication with those of our gallant fellow-countrymen whom we have been most anxious to assist.

No special record of cases suitable for Newington House is kept at the military headquarters in Edinburgh, nor can the committee in London, charged with the preparation of medical statistics supply, as yet, the requisite information; but a list was obtained from the authorities of Chelsea Hospital, of Scottish soldiers who have been discharged on pension on account of loss of eyesight.

It was found that most of these were already at St Dunstan's, but immediate steps were taken to communicate with the others who were not thus provided for, with the following results.

Private John Martin (34), Reservist of the Highland Light Infantry, was recalled to his Regiment at the beginning of the war. He fought at Mons and the Aisne and was then sent to Flanders. In November 1914 he was seriously wounded at Ypres by the bursting of a hand grenade. His face was cut, his lower jaw fractured, his right eye totally destroyed, and his left so seriously injured that a cataract formed in it, and even after this was extracted the eye remained for a long time irritable. And the vision so defective, that he was discharged from the Army as no longer fit for service. He came under my care after his return to Edinburgh, and underwent a further operation upon his surviving eye, with the happy result that now, with the aid of glasses, he is able to go about freely, and can read comparatively small print. As at one time there seemed a risk that his vision might not be so well restored, he was placed for a time under the care of Mr Stone, and received instruction in reading from Braille. Every effort was made to see that he was well cared for until he was able to maintain himself by sighted occupation. He now has charge of the rooms of the Australasian Students' club, where he resides with his wife and children.

Private Benjamin Mackenzie (30) of the Seaforth Highlanders was a farm labourer prior to his enlistment in July 1905. In December 1914 he was wounded at Neuve Chapelle upon the left side of the face by a piece of shell casing, which destroyed his left eye, and while still lying in the motor ambulance before leaving the firing line, he was struck by a shrapnel bullet behind the right ear. He was discharged from the Army as unfit for further service. The right side of his face was paralysed, and he could not close his eye properly. The left side of his face was greatly disfigured by the loss of the eye and eversion of the lower lid. A lady kindly visited him in Forres at my request, and he was invited by Mr Scott to come to Edinburgh, which he did, and was given accommodation at the Hostel. It was found that he had good enough vision in the right eye to enable him to pursue sighted occupation. He was admitted to the Deaconess Hospital, where I performed an operation which considerably diminished the disfigurement on the left side of his face. He was assisted to find employment with the Tramway Company.

Company Sergeant Major J E A Forsyth (31) comes of a family whose honourable tradition for generations has been to have at least one son in the Army. He was wounded at Loos, in the face, by a piece of shrapnel, and ten days later his right eye had to be removed. The left eye showed no appearance of damage externally, but unfortunately a haemorrhage into the retina, at the most sensitive area at the back of the eye, had greatly reduced its visual power, and necessitated his discharge from the Army. He was at once placed in communication with Mr Stone, who undertook his instruction in typewriting and being a man of quick intelligence, he has proved a most apt pupil. He is also at present engaged as Instructor in Physical Exercises at Craigmillar.

Private D Douglas lost his right eye by an accident in boyhood but managed to join the Army Service Corps in October 1915. He was employed as labourer on a boat on the river at Rouen, when he was injured by an explosion. Though a native of Leith, he was sent to St Margaret's Hospital, Chelsea, suffering from shock. He was then sent to the Catterick Camp in Yorkshire, and was discharged shortly after, suffering from heart weakness and greatly impaired vision. After that he was sent for a short time to St Dunstan's Training School. As his eyesight improved, he returned home to Leith. Here he was visited by Mr Stone, as well as examined by myself, and assisted to obtain occupation. He is now working with a relative on a farm in Galloway.

An offer of assistance was also made to Private J Kennedy, formerly of the Royal Scots, who now resides at Blairgowrie, but in the meantime, this has not been accepted, as he is unwilling to leave his wife and his home.

I have been enabled to place two other sufferers in communication with Mr Stone, but they are not yet able to avail themselves of the benefits offered to them. One is still in the Eye Wards of the Royal Infirmary here, and the other in the War Hospital at Bangour.

George Mackay. MD, FRCSE,
Ophthalmic Surgeon
17th October 1916

Great progress has been made in the development of this Scheme initiated by the Institution in 1915 for the purpose of training in Scotland and providing for blinded Scottish servicemen.

By arrangement with the Ministry of Pensions, Newington House has undertaken the training and aftercare of all Scotsmen who lose their sight in the service of their country, and the Pension Department has recognised Newington House as the Scottish National Institution for this purpose.

The Hostel is working in co-operation with St Dunstan's Hostel, London, and by arrangement with that Hostel, has undertaken the care of all men settled in Scotland who have been trained at St Dunstan's.

During the year the Hostel has been the means of benefiting many of our blinded heroes, and from present indications the available accommodation will soon all be required. Splendid work is being accomplished. The increased numbers have necessitated the provision of new workshops, and these are in course of erection in the grounds of Newington House.

The financial support has been generous, a sum of £18,971 having been received up to 30th September 1917. One of the happiest features has been the exceedingly generous support which Newington House has received from Scotsmen and Scotswomen abroad.

Very large sums in particular have been subscribed through Scottish Societies in America. But all the money which has been received, and much more, will be needed, for the care and employment of the men will be a lasting burden, extending over many years.

There has been great development in this branch of the Institution's work during the year. Commodious workshops have been erected and been in use for some time, and many new occupations for blinded servicemen have been introduced.

The men can now receive instruction in basket making, mat making, boot and shoe repairing, machine-knitting, net making, carpentry, poultry farming, piano tuning and music.

Poultry farming has been especially developed under the instruction of Miss Newbigin of the Edinburgh and East of Scotland College of Agriculture.

Two aftercare supervisors have been appointed and are taking charge of the men trained at St Dunstan's, or Newington House, who are settled in Scotland. This branch of the work will become more important as time progresses.

The aftercare of the many blinded Scotsmen will be a heavy undertaking and one which will make a steady call upon the funds which have been provided by Scotsmen, the world over, for their blinded.

A sum of £36,000 has been received up to 30th September, a splendid token of the loyalty of Scotsmen to this Scottish National Institution for the care of Scottish servicemen. Forty men have received instruction at Newington House during the year, and there are now 23 men under the charge of its aftercare department.

The work of the Hostel has been carried out during the year (1919) with great success. The accommodation has been taxed to the uttermost, but as a number of men have recently completed their training and been settled in homes of their own, the pressure has been somewhat relieved. Men, however, whose sight has been lost or impaired in the service of their country, are still coming forward for training, and there are at present 25 men under instruction at Newington House. Upwards of 70 men have received instruction or benefitted from Newington House - men from all parts of Scotland - from Stornoway and Inverness to Dumfries, from all Scottish Regiments, the Royal Field Artillery, Royal Garrison Artillery, Royal Engineers, Tanks, Army Service Corps, and Labour Corps. In different parts of Scotland men have been settled in poultry farms or in business. Other men have been returned to their homes to practice in a smaller way other trades and occupations. The Hostel provides each man with a sum of at least £150 to set him up on completing his training. There are two Aftercare Inspectors, who regularly visit the outside men and advise and help them in every way possible. The aftercare work will in due course of time become the more important part of the Hostel.

The total sum provided for the upkeep of the Hostel since the inception of the scheme, including all subscriptions, donations and legacies, and a grant from the National Relief Fund, amounts to £82,855.

On 21st November, 1918, His Majesty the King, who was accompanied by Her Majesty the Queen and HRH the Prince of Wales, honoured the work of the Hostel by arranging a stoppage at Salisbury Place in the course of his progress through the City, and addressing the men from the Hostel, who were drawn up to receive them.

Field Marshall Earl Haig and General Baron Horne also paid a visit to the Hostel on 29th May 1919. The visit gave great pleasure to the men. In the course of the year many others - official representatives and noblemen - visited the Hostel and were greatly delighted with the manner in which the men were cared for and trained at Newington House.

The work of this Institution has been carried on with much success in all Departments during the past six months. A good many men have completed their training during this period and have been satisfactorily settled in business on their own account.

Their places have been filled by others. There is still a steady influx of men whose sight has been so injured or impaired by the War that they are not able to follow ordinary sighted occupations. It was thought that as soon as the actual fighting stopped, the stream of sightless and disabled men would stop also.

But, alas, no; still they come! Happily, Newington House is able to deal with all blinded servicemen desiring admission, and it must be a great satisfaction to the subscribers to know that the necessary training is available in Scotland.

At 31st March there were 35 men under training at the Institution and Department.

Company Sergeant Major Robert Middlemiss, 2nd Kings Own Scottish Borderers, born at Edinburgh in 1880, he was the fifth son of John Middlemiss, a Dairy and Provision Merchant, and Catherine Gray Middlemiss, of 12 East Arthur Place, Edinburgh.

He enlisted at Edinburgh in 1898 and was medically discharged in 1915 when he was blinded by shrapnel during the Galipolli campaign. He then went to St Dunstan's to "Learn to be blind". In 1916, he was asked by the Permanent Blind Relief War Fund to go to America and Canada on a year-long lecture and fund-raising tour. On 3 May 1916, Robert and his wife, Beatrice, set sail for the USA on the SS Adriatic.

On the tour they met many influential statesmen, authors and actors and visited many cities including New York, Chicago, Cincinnati, Boston, Nashville, Cleveland and in Canada, Toronto. The Middlemiss' returned in May 1917.

Acknowledgements

Thanks to fellow veteran **George Tosh** for designing the front cover for this book and the also for the large print edition.

Thanks to **Evelyn** our tour guide for the notes and information that she helped me to collate.

Thanks to my eldest son **Aaron Jon (AJ) Mackie** for the majority of the photographs used in this book, that are copyright to him, which he took whilst accompanying me on the two tours mentioned in this book.

Special thanks to **Lt. Col. Colin Kemp,** my former Army Instructor, for writing the Foreword for this book.

To **Margaret Smith** and family for supplying the photograph of her mum, **Peggy Dunlop** at the start of this book.

Most especially, thanks to **Tim Searles** of the **Scottish War Blinded** for organising these trips for the members and their carer's.

Foreword

By

Lieutenant Colonel Colin Kemp (Retired)

Formerly Adjutant General's Corps (Staff and Personnel Support Branch) and
Royal Army Pay Corps

William K Mackie is a most interesting and self-disciplined person who appears to have dedicated his life towards self-improvement and the welfare of others through a multitude of disciplines. It will be seen from his later episodes in his search for discovery of his true self that he went on to master a great number of disciplines from a wide variety of unconnected subjects, which can be seen to have focused on people, welfare, truth and light. These disciplines included sailor, soldier, politician, comedian, criminologist, preacher, author, broadcaster, covenanter, and missionary.

I first met "Bill" Mackie in 1973 when he joined the Royal Army Pay Corps after serving in the Royal Navy. He was older than the average recruit when he joined the Army and, at times, was seen by his fellow soldiers as a mentor. I was his instructor for both his military and technical training phases and found him to be a reliable and inquisitive individual who had a high degree of respect for and the interest of others. He may have been seen by some as something of a barrack room lawyer due to his desire to see fairness, and in doing so he was prepared to, and on occasions did, politely challenge the decisions of those in charge, be they a non-commissioned officer or a fellow recruit in the role of duty student to good effect.

He went on to major as a preacher and travelled widely to learn from others as well as to share his views on his own and other religions. In recent years he started to lose his sight, then went on to research widely the lot of blinded and partially sighted military personnel in particular. I feel sure his interest in and devotion to this field inspired others to contribute in various ways towards support for those whose sight had been affected by military service and, as he anticipated the possibility of being blinded eventually, he saw the need and value of large print publications for those who are, or would become, partially sighted.

In writing "Echoes Through Time" he has demonstrated the lengths to which he has been prepared to go in all of his projects, devoting time and energy towards obtaining and verifying the facts about his chosen subjects before going to print.

"Echoes Through Time" in large print form can be more easily read by those with either normal or impaired vision, but particularly for those with impaired vision. The recollections of Mackie's own visits to war graves, cemeteries and battle scenes provide the reader with sufficient information to understand the detail and battle history of the locations visited for them to be satisfied by merely reading the book, whilst for other readers "Echoes Through Time" may well encourage and inspire them to seek an opportunity for themselves to actually visit the sites covered by the book, as well as other battlefields and cemeteries in Western Europe and beyond.

Contents

Part One

World War One Battlefields

Day One

Tyne Cot

We travelled to Zeebrugge by ferry, and once we had departed Zeebrugge we travelled to Tyne Cot Commonwealth War Graves Cemetery. Tyne Cot is the largest Commonwealth War Graves Cemetery in the world.

Prior to our departure from Linburn, I had been asked if I could possibly keep an audio diary of the entire trip. I agreed and was all set to do just that as we stepped off the bus and walked into the cemetery. It was not until I walked through the gates of this cemetery that it hit me.

As I walked in through the gates this was the scene that greeted me. There are over 11,954 servicemen either buried here or have their names and regiments etc. engraved on several panels around the walls.

It was at this point that I decided to take notes of what I saw and then dictate these notes later. The end result was the creation of a YouTube presentation.

Tyne Cot got its name as a result of men from the Northumberland Fusiliers, who on first seeing this part of the Western Front remarked at home the houses that we there at the time looked very much like Tyne Cottages back home.

Zonnebeke Memorial Museum Passchendaele.

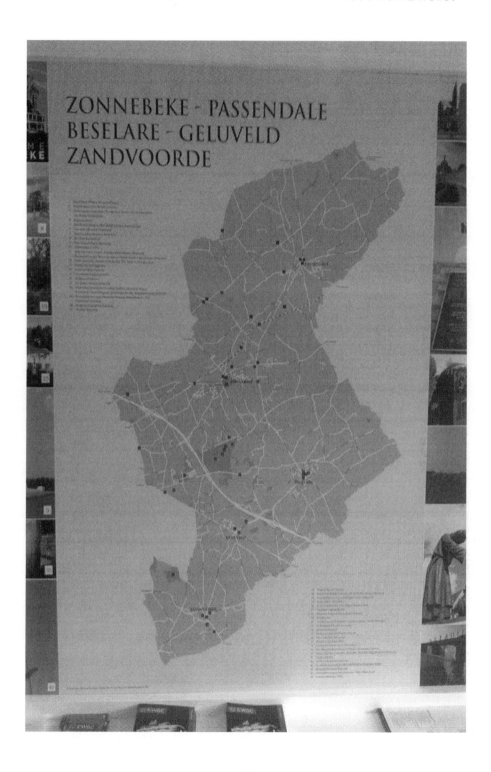

As you can see from the following pictures the Scottish Regiments played an important part Battle for Passchendaele.

The picture above shows the kilt of the Gordon Highlanders.

This picture shows three glengarries of Scottish Regiments. They are (L to R), The Royal Scots, The King's Own Scottish Borders and the Gordon Highlanders.

Scottish National Monument

We then went on to visit the Scottish National Monument which was dedicated to ALL Scottish servicemen who fought and died during WW1.

The monument has since become a popular magnet for pilgrims to the war graves in Belgium.

In August 2007, to mark the 90th anniversary of the battle of Passchendaele, a memorial was unveiled at Frezenberg Hill near Zonnebeke, Flanders. Hewn from solid Scottish granite the impressive Celtic cross was raised by public subscription in memory Scots and those of Scots descent who lost their lives in the battle of Passchendaele.

Ten years on, crowds gathered for the 100th Anniversary of the Scottish advance on Passchendaele ridge. Once again, the general public, as well as a range of organisations in Flanders, Scotland and beyond, supported an initiative to further preserve the memory of soldiers who never came home. Soldiers from all walks of life, who answered the nations call and paid the ultimate sacrifice.

For the centennial commemorations, the memorial site has been enhanced with the erection of ten silhouettes depicting soldiers advancing on the Western Front. Constructed from COR-TEN steel which forms a stable rust-like preserving film, the 150% life-size figures provide an unmissable, stark reflection of a time of battle. One of the silhouettes depicts a piper, evoking the role of the Scottish bagpipes in the war as a means to rally troops as well as to lament the fallen.

The unveiling was part of a themed weekend of 18-20 August 2017, in and around Passchendaele when visitors, dignitaries and war-grave pilgrims gathered to take part in events to mark 100 years since the Scottish advance in what became one of the bloodiest battles on the western front.

Representatives from Scotland, Australia, New Zealand, Canada and South Africa as well as from the local Flanders community, attended to pay their respects to those of Scottish descent who served among the Scottish diaspora.

This memorial is the only one on the former Western Front dedicated to all Scots and all those of Scottish descent who fought in France and Flanders during WWI. It is now the main site of remembrance activities for all Scots. This memorial also remembers those men of the South African Brigade who, throughout the war, fought with the Scots as part of the 9th (Scottish) Division.

Scots and the Great War

It is estimated that over a quarter of all Scots who fought in the Great War were killed, but Scotland's role and suffering in the First World War was not unique. Her experience of war was similar to all the other countries that were fighting.

However, the way in which people in Scotland reacted to the war was distinctive. The reasons why people fought and the way in which the pressures of war help to make a unique story. The Scottish people coped heroically but were changed forever in how they looked at themselves and their country.

One of the biggest changes was in how people chose to remember the war and those who died. There is hardly a town or village in Scotland that does not have a memorial to those who died. The work of raising memorials began almost as soon as the war had ended. As Scotland came to terms with the human cost of the Great War, people's grief for their dead loved ones only seemed to grow.

By the beginning of the 20th Century, Scots no longer fought in the army in the same numbers that they once had done. However, the symbols of the Scottish military history – the kilt, the Highland traditions and the bagpipes – continued to be important to the Scottish identity. Especially in the rural areas, plus being part of a local territorial force was an important part of community life. The sense of a shared history as well as membership of the territorial forces helped to boost recruitment at the start of the Great War.

The impact of the Scots on the fighting of the Great War is sometimes hard to access because Scottish soldiers fought as part of the British Army. Not only that, but as the war went on, even regiments that had strong Scottish ties increasingly had to be recruit from within the British Isles to replace casualties. It is, however, still possible to see the importance of the Scots at certain points in the Great War. They had a real impact at the beginning of the war as regular Scottish Battalions were part of the British Expeditionary Force (BEF) who fought with particular bravery at Mons / Le Cateau.

The Scots were important as attack troops and they played a significant role in the battles of Loos, the Somme, Arras and Cambrai. This fact was reflected in the casualty figures; in relative terms Scotland lost more of its troops from actual fighting than any other nation. The Scottish battalions were highly visible; whenever the kilted regiments fought, they received a great deal of attention.

At the time there was a huge feeling that Scotland had "punched above its weight" in its contribution to the fighting. This is one reason why Scotland made its own. National War Memorial. Perhaps most distinctively Scotland contributed to the general who commanded the British troops to victory. His role however has been seen as being controversial, but Haig was the commander who had the realism and tenacity required to win such a mammoth industrial war. These qualities were reflected in the service and experience of his fellow Scots.

This picture shows General Haigh (right) with King George V

Essex Farm

Our third port of call was to the Grave site known as Essex Farm where there is a memorial to the late Lt. Col. John McCrae, who whilst serving here on 3rd May 1915, wrote the famous poem "In Flanders Field."

The picture below shows the medical bunker, where Army medics and nurses would dress and asses the wounds of those injured in battle.

The Menin Gate

As with the walls at Tyne Cot Cemetery, the Walls of the Menin Gate
Has the names of 54,395 soldiers for whom there are "No known graves."

Ypres occupied a strategic position during the First World War because it stood in the path of Germany's planned sweep across the rest of Belgium, as had been called for in the Schlieffen Plan. By October 1914, the much-battered Belgian Army broke the dykes on the Yser River to the north of the City to keep the western tip of Belgium out of German hands. Ypres, being the centre of a road network, anchored one end of this defensive feature and was also essential for the Germans if they wanted to take the Channel Ports through which British support was flooding into France. For the Allies, Ypres was also important because it eventually became the last major Belgian town that was not under German control.

The importance of the town is reflected in the five major battles that occurred around it during the war. During the First Battle of Ypres the Allies halted the German Army's advance to the east of the city. The German army eventually surrounded the city on three sides, bombarding it throughout much of the war. The Second Battle of Ypres marked a second German attempt to take the city in April 1915. The third battle is more commonly referred to as Passchendaele, but this 1917 battle was a complex five-month engagement. The fourth and fifth battles occurred during 1918.

British and Commonwealth soldiers often passed through the Menenpoort on their way to the front lines with some 300,000 of them being killed in the Ypres Salient. 90,000 of these soldiers have no known graves.

From September to November 1915, the British 177th Tunnelling Company built tunnelled dugouts in the city ramparts near the Menin Gate. These were the first British tunnelled dugouts in the Ypres Salient.

The carved limestone lions adorning the original gate were damaged by shellfire and were donated to the Australian War Memorial by the Mayor of Ypres in 1936. They were restored in 1987, and currently reside at the entrance to that Memorial, so that all visitors to the Memorial pass between them.

A friend of the late Queen Elizabeth the Queen Mother found the name of her one of her brothers who died in the Great War. On hearing the news, the Queen Mother contacted the Commonwealth Graves Commission to give them the exact burial place of her brother. His name has since been deleted from the Menin Gate wall.

The Menin Gate Ceremony is carried out nightly throughout the year.

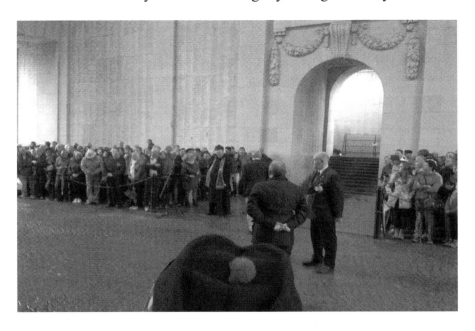

Day Two

Lochnagar Crater

We set out from our hotel and made our way to the Lochnagar Crater.

The Lochnagar Crater was created by a large mine placed beneath the German front lines on the first day of the Battle of the Somme, it was one of 19 mines that were placed beneath the German lines from the British section of the Somme front, to assist the infantry advance at the start of the battle.

The British named the mine after 'Lochnagar Street', a British trench where the Tunnelling Companies of the Royal Engineers dug a shaft down about 90 feet deep into the chalk; then excavated some 300 yards towards the German lines to place 60,000 lbs (27 tons) of ammonal explosive in two large adjacent underground chambers 60 feet apart. Its aim was to destroy a formidable strongpoint called 'Schwaben Höhe' (Swabian Heights) in the German front line, south of the village of La Boisselle in the Somme département.

On Saturday 1st July 1916, at 7.28am, two minutes before the attack began, the mine was exploded, leaving the massive crater 70ft (21m) deep and 330 ft (100 m) wide, that we see today.

Debris was flung almost a mile into the air, as graphically recorded by Royal Flying Corps pilot Cecil Lewis in his book 'Sagittarius Rising': 'The whole earth heaved and flared, a tremendous and magnificent column rose up into the sky. There was an ear-splitting roar, drowning all the guns, flinging the machine sideways in the repercussing air. The earth column rose higher and higher to almost 4,000 feet.'

The reason the Crater is so large is that the chambers were overcharged. Meaning, sufficient explosive was used to, not only break the surface and form a crater, but enough to cause spoil to fall in the surrounding fields and form a lip around the Crater of approximately 15ft high, to protect the advancing British troops from enfilade machine-gun fire from the nearby village of La Boisselle.

The Crater was captured and held by British troops but the attack on either flank was defeated by German small-arms and artillery fire – except on the extreme right flank and between La Boisselle and the Lochnagar Crater.

Today the Lochnagar Crater has been preserved as a memorial to all the men and women of all nations who suffered in the Great War and now has in excess of 200,000 visits a year, many of them British and French schoolchildren.

In 1986 a large cross of medieval wood was erected close to the lip. It was made with roof timbers from an abandoned, deconsecrated church close to Durham – most likely a church used by some of the soldiers from Tyneside who themselves fell at Lochnagar.

On the anniversary on July 1st, a remembrance ceremony is held, starting at 7.28am – the exact time of the explosion. Lasting about an hour, with around 75 wreaths being laid, it is often attended by up to 1,000 people.

This picture shows an aerial view of what the Lochnagar Crater today.
It is said that the noise of the craters exploding was so loud, that they could hear the explosion in London.

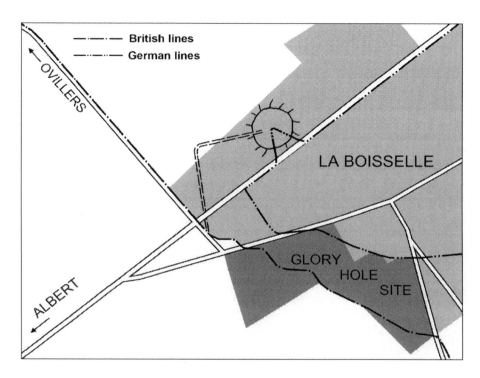

Maps of the area where most of the fighting took place on July 1st. 1916

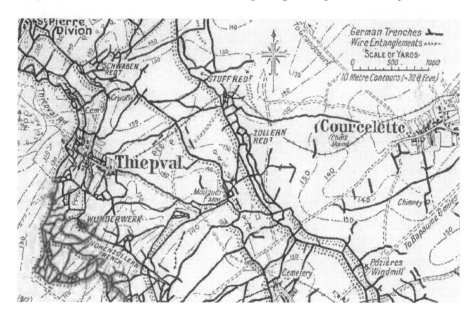

It was such a cold day that my son AJ offered to get hots drinks for some of our members from the tea shack in the background.

Looking down into the crater.

Thiepval Memorial

Our second port of call on day two was to the largest memorial to British and Commonwealth troops anywhere in the world, Thiepval Memorial to the missing of the Somme.

During the Battle of the Somme 1.3 million soldiers lost their lives. This Monument at Thiepval is the largest War Memorial to British and Commonwealth dead outside of mainland Britain. The foundation is 20 metres underground and the monument stands some 45 metres high. The cemetery has both French and British Empire graves. For the most part French and German dead were gathered and buried in large communal graves.

As with Tyne Cot there are panels on this monument that bear the names of 73,367 Commonwealth soldiers with no known resting place. Also like at Tyne Cote and the other War graves we visited too the majority of headstones have no name just "A Soldier of the Great War" "Known unto GOD"

The French Graves have crosses, not headstones.

The picture above shows the crosses making graves of soldiers whose remains were found after the battle. French troops on the left with wooden crosses, and British and Commonwealth troops with white headstones.

This picture shows one of the many walls containing the names of those who died in battle but whose bodies were never found.

Auchonvillers

We then moved off to have our lunch at Auchonvillers, where there is a Commonwealth War Graves Cemetery and museum.

We later had our lunch at the rear of the Museum.

The British Tommy had problems pronouncing Auchonvillers so instead they called it "Ocean Villas"

Beaumont Hammel, Newfoundland Park.

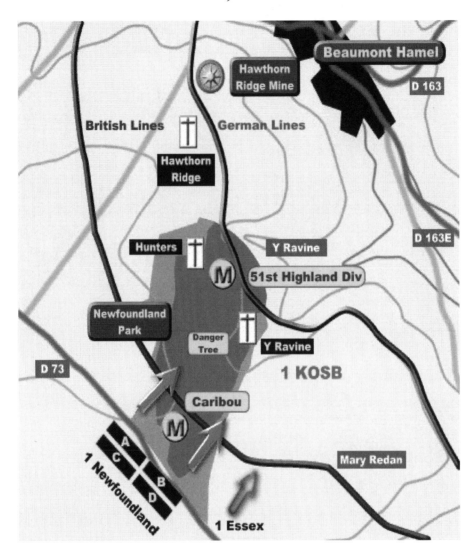

When you first approach the Beaumont Hammel, Newfoundland Park the first thing to catch your eye is an amazing Caribou standing on top of a hill made entirely from rocks that were shipped in especially from Newfoundland. The battlefield still has many of the original trenches left to give the visitor an idea of the lay of the land during the fighting.

Although the Newfoundland Park now flies the Canadian "Maple Leaf" flag, and although the entire park is manned by Canadian Students, you might cause offence to say that this was a Canadian battlefield. In fact, at the time of the Great War, Newfoundland was not part of the Canadian Nation.

The magnificent Caribou standing guard on top of stones taken from Newfoundland.

There are many memorials and plaques around the Newfoundland Park.

Not all of those who fought and died were from Newfoundland, and not all were soldiers.

As you can see from the picture above there were many soldiers from Scottish Regiments who fought and died in the fighting at Beaumont Hammel.

The picture above shows that some gravestones have two Regimental crests on them. This is because the soldiers whilst of different Regiments, died side by side, but as there was not enough remains to give each soldier a grave to themselves, they were buried as they died, together.

This plaque shows that it was not just soldiers who fought and died at Beaumont Hammel. The picture above lists the names of those of the Newfoundland Mercantile Marine who died in battle here.

Day Three

Ploegsteert

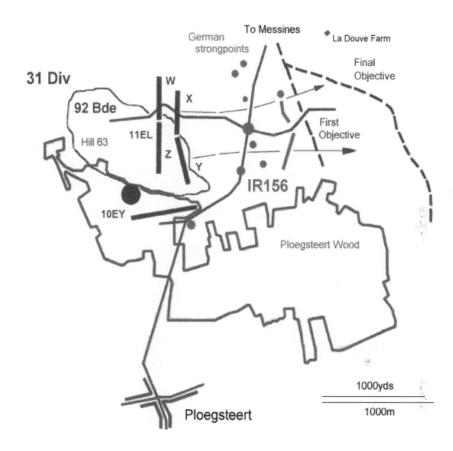

Ploegsteert Wood was a sector of the Western Front in Flanders in World War I, part of the Ypres Salient. It is located around the village of Ploegsteert in the Walloon region of north-western Belgium.

After fierce fighting in late 1914 and early 1915, Ploegsteert Wood became a quiet sector where no major action took place. Units were sent here to recuperate and retrain after tougher fighting elsewhere and before returning to take part in more active operations. British Tommies referred to Ploegsteert Wood as "Plugstreet Wood". From January to May 1916, Winston Churchill served in the area as Commanding Officer (Lieutenant-Colonel) of the 6th Battalion of the Royal Scots Fusiliers.

There are numerous Commonwealth War Graves Commission (CWGC) cemeteries and memorials around the wood, including the Hyde Park Corner

(Royal Berks) CWGC Cemetery and the Berks CWGG Cemetery Extension with the Ploegsteert Memorial to the Missing. The Ploegsteert Memorial commemorates more than 11,000 British and Empire servicemen who died during the First World War and have no known grave. It is one of several CWGC Memorials to the Missing along the Western Front. Those lost within the Ypres Salient without a known grave are commemorated at the Menin Gate and Tyne Cot Memorial to the Missing, while the missing of New Zealand and Newfoundland are honoured on separate memorials.

Citation: An extract from "The London Gazette," dated 4th Aug. 1916, records the following: -"For most conspicuous bravery when entombed with four others in a gallery owing to the explosion of an enemy mine. After working for 20 hours, a hole was made through fallen earth and broken timber, and the outside party was met. Sapper Hackett helped three of the men through the hole and could easily have followed, but refused to leave the fourth, who had been seriously injured, saying," I am a tunneller, I must look after the others first." Meantime, the hole was getting smaller, yet he still refused to leave his injured comrade. Finally, the gallery collapsed, and though the rescue party worked desperately for four days the attempt to reach the two men failed. Sapper Hackett well knowing the nature of sliding earth, the chances against him, deliberately gave his life for his comrade".

Citation: An extract from "The London Gazette," dated 16th Feb., 1915, records the following:-"For conspicuous bravery at Rouges Bancs on the 19th Dec., in rescuing a severely wounded man from in front of the German trenches, under a very heavy fire and after a stretcher-bearer party had been compelled to abandon the attempt. Private Mackenzie was subsequently killed on that day whilst in the performance of a similar act of gallant conduct."

Citation: An extract from "The London Gazette," dated 21st May 1918, records the following-"For most conspicuous bravery, devotion to duty, and self-sacrifice when in command of a flank on the left of the Grenadier Guards. Having been ordered to attack a village he personally led forward two platoons, working from house to house, killing some thirty of the enemy, seven of whom he killed himself. The next day he was occupying a position with some thirty to forty men, the remainder of his company having become casualties. As early as 8.15 a.m., his left flank was surrounded, and the enemy was enfilading him. He was attacked no less than four times during the day, and each time beat off the hostile attack, killing many of the enemy. Meanwhile the enemy brought three field guns to within 300 yards of his line, and were firing over open sights and knocking his trench in. At 6.15 p.m., the enemy had worked to within sixty yards of his trench. He then called on his men, telling them to cheer and charge the enemy and fight to the last. Led by Captain Pryce, they left their trench and drove back the enemy

with the bayonet some 100 yards. Half an hour later the enemy had again approached in stronger force. By this time Captain Pryce had only 17 men left, and every round of his ammunition had been fired. Determined that there should be no surrender, he once again led his men forward in a bayonet charge and was last seen engaged in a fierce hand-to-hand struggle with overwhelming numbers of the enemy. With some forty men he had held back at least one enemy battalion for over ten hours. His company undoubtedly stopped the advance through the British line, and thus had great influence on the battle."

As with so many Commonwealth War Graves there are many panels with the names of soldiers known to have died but for whom there is no known resting place.

As was the case on many parts of the Western Ploegsteert was the scene of one of the Christmas Truce football matches. See the map on page 51 the area Ploegtseert Woods

The future Prime Minister Winston Churchill was not the only soldier of note to have served at Ploegtseert, Corporal Adolf Hitler was fighting on the other side of the battlefield, but not it is thought at the same time Churchill.

The church in the picture above is reported to be where Corporal Hitler was taken for treatment after having a testicle shot off during battle. So perhaps the World War II song was more than just a jibe at the leader of the Third Reich.

"Island of Ireland Peace Park."

From Ploegtseert we travelled a short distance along the road towards Ypres, where we came upon the "Island of Ireland Peace Park."

This monument was not erected until after the Good Friday agreement which was signed by both the British and the Republic of Ireland Governments.

The Island of Ireland Peace Park and its surrounding park, also called the Irish Peace Park or Irish Peace Tower in Messines, near Ypres in Flanders, Belgium, is a war memorial to the soldiers of the island of Ireland who died, were wounded or are missing from World War I, during Ireland's involvement in the conflict. The tower memorial is close to the site of the June 1917 battle of Messines Ridge, during which the 16th (Irish) Division fought alongside the 36th (Ulster) Division.

Because of the events of the Easter Rebellion in 1916 and the partition of Ireland under the Anglo-Irish Treaty in 1922 and the Irish Civil War that followed it, little was done in the Republic of Ireland to commemorate the Irish dead from the Great War or World War II. Those countries who were engaged in the Great War all preserve the memory of their fallen soldiers with national monuments in the

Western Front area. This led to some ill-feeling in the already crowded emotions of the conflict on the island, and perhaps was highlighted when Northern Ireland's community's Ulster Tower Thiepval in France was one of the first memorials erected.

This Tower memorial, however, serves not to "redress the balance" but rather to recall the sacrifices of those from the island of Ireland from all political and religious traditions who fought and died in the war. It also serves as a symbol of modern-day reconciliation. The Tower houses bronze cubicles containing record books listing the known dead, which are publicly accessible copies of the originals belonging to the National War Memorial, Island Bridge, Dublin.

The project was initiated by a member of the Irish Parliament (Dail Eireann), Paddy Harte TD, who, together with a community activist, Glen Barr from Northern Ireland, established 'A Journey of Reconciliation Trust'. The Trust was a broad-based, cross-border, organisation with offices in Dublin. The Trust was made up of representatives of the main churches in Ireland and professional political and representatives and community leaders from both parts of Ireland under the leadership of Paddy Harte and Glenn Barr.

The Irish government became involved in part funding the project together with the Northern Ireland Office. Statutory and private bodies rolled in behind the project and within two years of the initiation of the JRT the Island of Ireland Peace Park and Celtic Round tower was complete.

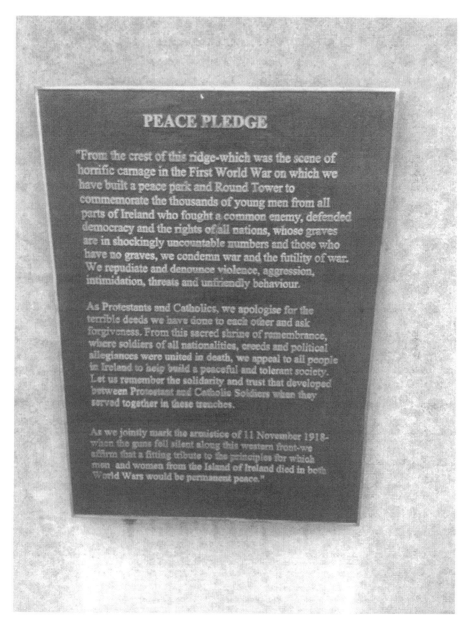

It was formally opened by the Irish President Mary McAleese who in the presence of Queen Elizabeth and King Albert of Belgium led the wreath laying ceremony in the afternoon of 11th of November 1998. It was the first time an Irish State officially acknowledged the soldiers from Ireland who died in WW1. This was also a seminal moment in Irish history when an Irish Head of State and a British Monarch met publicly in a joint ceremony. The Park is maintained by the Commonwealth War Graves Commission on behalf of the Office of Public Works in Ireland. Prior to the Island of Ireland Peace Park, no Irish government dignitary had ever attended any WW1 Remembrance Service either in Ireland or at the Menin Gate. At an official ceremony on 11th November 1998 the Irish President apologised on behalf of the Republic of Ireland to the families of the fallen for what she called the 'national amnesia' in remembering the soldiers of WW1 from the Island of Ireland.

The 110-foot (34 m) tower is in the traditional design of an Irish round tower and is partially built with stone from a former British Army barracks in Tipperary, the remainder of the stone from a workhouse outside Mullingar, County Westmeath.

The design has a unique aspect that allows the sun to light the interior only on the 11th hour of the 11th day of the 11th month, the anniversary of the armistice that ended the war and the time for the minute's silence on Remembrance Day.

A commemorative ceremony is held yearly in the park on Armistice Day in conjunction with similar ceremonies at the nearby multi-national Menin Gate Memorial in Ypres.

The tower was unveiled in the afternoon on 11 November 1998 by President Mary McAleese of Ireland, Queen Elizabeth II of the United Kingdom and King Albert II of Belgium.

In her speech, **President McAleese** said:

"Today's ceremony at the Peace Park was not just another journey down a well-travelled path. For much of the past eighty years, the very idea of such a ceremony would probably have been unthinkable.

Those whom we commemorate here were doubly tragic. They fell victim to a war against oppression in Europe. Their memory too fell victim to a war for independence at home in Ireland."

Speaking at the Park on the anniversary of the Battle of Messines Ridge on 7 June 2004, the Irish Minister for Foreign Affairs Dermot Ahern commented that honouring the spirit of the Irish killed in the First World War can teach how to advance the Northern Ireland peace process in Northern Ireland, adding:

"All those untold human stories that we lost in the First World War and more recently in the conflict in Northern Ireland, must be remembered. And, in remembering, they must not be told for nothing. They must not be told to deepen divisions. They must be told to inspire us to overcome them." Dermot Ahern

A bronze tablet on a granite pillar positioned in the centre circle of the park bears the following inscription: (See page 61).

Peace Pledge

"From the crest of this ridge, which was the scene of terrific carnage in the First World War on which we have built a peace park and Round Tower to commemorate the thousands of young men from all parts of Ireland who fought a common enemy, defended democracy and the rights of all nations, whose graves are in shockingly uncountable numbers and those who have no graves, we condemn war and the futility of war. We repudiate and denounce violence, aggression, intimidation, threats and unfriendly behaviour.

As Protestants and Catholics, we apologise for the terrible deeds we have done to each other and ask forgiveness. From this sacred shrine of remembrance, where soldiers of all nationalities, creeds and political allegiances were united in death, we appeal to all people in Ireland to help build a peaceful and tolerant society. Let us remember the solidarity and trust that developed between Protestant and Catholic soldiers when they served together in these trenches.

As we jointly thank the armistice of 11 November 1918 – when the guns fell silent along this western front - we affirm that a fitting tribute to the principles for which men and women from the Island of Ireland died in both World Wars would be permanent peace.

"In Flanders Field Museum."

Our last stop on this tour before heading back to the ferry at Zeebrugge, was to the "In Flanders Field Museum."

Sadly, the tour guides had not really thought this visit through given that most of those on our coach had some degree of Visual Impairment.

When we first entered into the Museum it was well lit up and it was a very large building.

We were all issued with a wrist band with a Poppy design on it, (see page 67) this wrist band allowed us access to all areas of the museum.

To enter the actual exhibits, we had to take the escalator up to the first floor (second if you live across the pond).

The Poppy wrist bands.

Once we reached the entry level to the displays and used our wrist bands to get through the turnstile, we discovered that it was almost all in darkness, and that the floor was anything but flat with steps and ramps at various points throughout the tour. So sadly, most of us had to return to the ground floor where we purchased gifts from the Museum Shop and had coffee and cake into Café.

We went out onto the market square in search of the Peter De Groot Chocolate Shop, where, by telling them which tour company we were with we were each given a selection of the chocolate products the make, and we paid only €10.00 per person.

We then made our way towards the Menin gate where our coach was waiting to take us home.

This picture shows the members, staff of the Scottish War Blinded as well as members' carers who came on this journey as we stepped back through the echoes of time, to visit Battlefields of the Great War.

Key Battles involving Scottish Regiments

It is somewhat difficult to assess the distinctive contribution of the Scots to the fighting of the First World War because they fought as part of the British Army. However, in the battles detailed below, we know that large members of Scots were involved. Sadly, as the war progressed and casualty rates rose, battalions had to be recruited from across the United Kingdom, Scottish Regiments raised in their own geographical areas, such as the Gordon Highlanders normally recruiting in Aberdeenshire, much more mixed.

For example:

The picture above is of Lt. Basil Rathbone who enlisted in the
Liverpool Scottish Regiment

The Battle of Loos.

This was part of a series of battles by the allies to attack the large German salient which ran from Flanders to Verdun. The French would attack from the South and the British would attack from the North.

- The British were involved in the battles of Neuve Chapelle, Aubers Ridge, Festubert and Loos.

- Loos involved the first of Lord Kitchener's New Army Divisions

- Scottish losses were so dreadful that no part of Scotland went unaffected. The Black Watch (raised in Tayside) had massive casualties; the 9th. Lost 680 officers and men in the first hours of battle. Of the 950 6th. Cameronians who went into battle, 700 were casualties.

- It was a relatively meaningless battle in regard to what it achieved. Joint French-British offensive. Haig was sceptical owing to the lack of artillery and introduction of new army units. He was overruled by Kitchener. Haig felt he did not have enough men and his reserves were far behind the front line. Gas was to be used to make up for the lack of artillery.

- Loos deserves to be called a Scottish battle because of the large number of Scottish troops that took part in the action. 30,000 Scots took part in the attack.

- Of the 72 infantry battalions taking part in the first phase of the battle, half of them were Scottish.

- They came up against fierce German opposition organised in strong points such as the Hohenzollern Redoubt, Fosse 8 and hill 70.

- The attack broke down owing to German reinforcement of their position and the time that it took to get reserve units up to support the limited success of the first day.

- In total there were five Victoria Crosses awarded to Scots in recognition of their extraordinary bravery.

- Of the 20598 names of the dead on the memorial at Loos one-third are Scottish.

- There was a bloody-minded attitude among the survivors: losses were replaced, and the Scottish units got back to the job in hand.

The Somme

Three Scottish Divisions – 9th, 15th (Scottish) and 51st. (Highland) – took part as well as numerous Scottish Battalions in other units including the Scots Guards of the Household Division.

- Douglas Haigh, an Edinburgh born Scot, had been made their Commander-in-Chief by this time.

- It was Haigh's intension to attack the Germans with an overwhelming force. His plan was to break through their lines and take over the reserve areas.

- A week long bombardment from 1000 guns and a creeping barrage would mean that British soldiers would able to walk through the German lines, or so it was hoped. German lines were well prepared, and the British armies suffered horrendous casualties; 57480 o the first day alone.

- Examples of Scottish losses on the first day:
  15th. (Cranstons) Royal Scots lost 18 officers and 610 soldiers were wounded, killed or missing.
  16th. (McCraes) Royal Scots lost 12 officers and 573 soldiers
  16th. Highland Light Infantry lost 20 officers and 534 soldiers
  51st. Highland Division suffered 3500 casualties following two attacks on an objective called High Wood.

- Despite losses there was still a belief in victory, but some criticism of war and its slaughter began.

- Successes, however, did also exist. For instance, the 51st. (Highland) Division launched a successful attack at Beaumont Hammel with very few casualties in November 1918.

- We must pay tribute to the attitude of the Scottish Soldier. Three platoons of the 16th. Highland Light Infantry were isolated after an attack on a trench called Frankfurt Trench. They held out for a whole 8 days against ferocious German attacks. There was absolutely no value in their doing so, but it spoke volumes as to their attitude.

British soldiers being taken from the battlefield have suffered as the result of a gas attack.

- There were some 400,000 casualties

- The Somme was seen by many to be a win on points despite the slaughter of so many for so little being gained. German commanders after the war felt that the Battle of the Somme had seen the death of the German field army. As for the Scottish units, they learned the lessons of the battle despite their sacrifice.

- The 9th. (Scottish) Division performed well during the five months of fighting. Casualties were high – 314 officers and 7203 other ranks – yet morale remained high.

General Haigh inspecting Scottish soldiers

Arras 1917

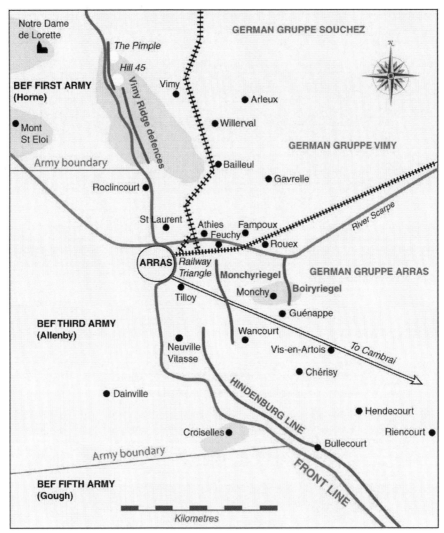

Red line = front line on April 9, 1917
Green lines = Major German trench systems / defensive lines
Blue line = River Scarpe

- This battle saw the concentration of 44 Scottish Battalions and seven Scottish named Canadian Battalions attacking on the first day, making it the largest concentration of Scots to have fought together.

- This included soldiers from 9th. (Scottish), 15th. (Scottish), 51st. (Highland) Divisions as well as the battalions from other divisions.

- Despite the initial assault being very successful, sadly localised losses, the impetus was lost. The German resistance stiffened, and their reserves were brought up. Bad weather and the failure of the French "Nivelle" offensive did not help the allied cause.

- One third of the 159,000 British casualties were Scottish

- Scottish units were also involved in the Third Battle of Ypres and at Cambrai.

Trivia:

Did you know that the first and last shots of World War 1 both took place in Africa. The first shot fired was in Togoland, now know as Togo in West Africa. At the time Togoland was a German Colony. The last shot to be fired in World War 1 was fired (on 25th November 1918, a full two weeks after the end of hostilities in Europe) in Tanganyika, now known as Tanzania, which at the time was also colonised by Germany.

The woman who fought as a man in the trenches

She fought on the Somme disguised as a Tommy, so why did Dorothy die unloved and unlauded in a lunatic asylum? Incredible story of the only British woman to fight in the trenches.

In Paris, in the high summer of 1915, Dorothy Lawrence – a young Englishwoman with more by way of courage and ambition than wealth or connections – turned herself into a Tommy.

She flattened her hourglass curves with a home-made corset stuffed with cotton-wool, hacked off her long, brown hair and darkened her complexion with Condy's Fluid, a disinfectant made from potassium permanganate. She even razored the pale skin of her cheeks in the hope of giving herself a shaving rash.

In a borrowed military uniform she disguised the last vestiges of her female shape and found two British soldiers to teach her to walk like a man. She completed her transformation by forging her own bona fides and travel permits for war-ravaged France and caught a train to Amiens.

And then Dorothy Lawrence, a cub reporter who hungered to be a war correspondent, cycled to Albert, the village known as the front of the Front, and joined the ranks of 179 Tunnelling Company, 51st Division, Royal Engineers, as they dug beneath no-man's-land and across to German lines.

They kept her presence a secret. 'You don't know what danger you are in,' Sapper Tommy Dunn warned her, meaning from the battle-hardened, woman-starved men of her own side, not the enemy mortars.

What he could not have known was the terrible secret which had driven Dorothy to take such risks. Ten years later she would reveal she had been raped as a child by the 'highly respected' church guardian who had raised her after she was orphaned.

For almost two weeks in August 1915, Dorothy toiled in the sniper-infested trenches of the Somme – which a year later were to erupt in the bloody hell immortalised by the Sebastian Faulks novel Birdsong – until, weakened by contaminated water and exhaustion, she revealed herself to be a female civilian to her 'superiors'.

She knew she had the scoop of her life, a story which would set Fleet Street alight.

Even when the British military locked her in a convent to keep her quiet in the final days before the Battle of Loos the following month, she was confident it would make her name.

Emmeline Pankhurst, leader of the Suffragettes, agreed. After a chance encounter on the ferry home, she invited Dorothy to lecture the growing ranks of women desperate to contribute to Britain's war effort. But Dorothy was banned by the War Office from telling her inspirational story either through newspaper articles or talks until after the Armistice in 1918.

By the time her book, Sapper Dorothy Lawrence, The Only English Woman Soldier, appeared in 1919 it was well received in England, America and Australia, but remaindered within a year as a world exhausted by war looked ahead to the glamour of the Roaring Twenties.

It left Dorothy with neither reputation nor income, and by 1925 she was living in rented rooms in Islington, North London, her behaviour increasingly erratic. With no family to look after her, she was taken into care, and committed first to the London County Mental Hospital and then Colney Hatch Lunatic Asylum.

It was here she revealed the tragedy of her broken childhood to doctors – but there is no evidence her allegations were taken seriously and investigated as they would be today.

It is even possible she was declared insane because she dared to air them publicly. A century ago the word of a man of the Church would have been believed over that of a woman capable of something The Spectator described in its September 1919 review of her book as a 'girlish freak'.

Dorothy was in hospital for a shocking 39 years until her lonely death in the asylum in 1964. She was buried in a pauper's grave in New Southgate Cemetery, where the site of her plot is no longer clear.

It was a tragic end to what could have been a brilliant life in the vanguard of women's journalism. Today, however, as Britain prepares to mark the centenary of the First World War, her exploits are finally being applauded.

Military historian Simon Jones stumbled across a copy of her long-forgotten book while working at the Royal Engineers Museum in Chatham, Kent, ten years ago and is now writing her biography.

With his help, The Mail on Sunday has pieced together fragments of Dorothy's personal and professional life – and can reveal for the first time that her rape allegations were sufficiently compelling to be included in her medical records, held in the London Metropolitan Archives.

'At the time she was committed her account of the rape was seen as manic behaviour, delusional, but if it was true it might go some way to explaining why she did what she did,' Simon says.

'We know today that victims of sexual abuse do not value their own wellbeing – did Dorothy deliberately put herself in danger? If she understood the danger she was in, she did not seem to fear it. Albert in those days was somewhere soldiers tried to avoid – they would even deliberately injure themselves – yet she headed straight for it.'

Simon has, however, been frustrated by the mysteries of Dorothy's early and later life.

Her adventures in 1915 are clearly told – although he believes they benefit from a bit of spin – but her early years remain an enigma and, as a mental patient, little is known about her from 1925 onwards.

He believes she was born in Hendon, North London, at the end of the 1880s to an unmarried mother who used several aliases.

When her mother died, Dorothy – then aged around 13 or 14 – was handed into the care of a churchman. Dorothy describes him as 'highly respected' and says she was raised in 'one of England's cathedral cities'. Simon has traced this to South-West England.

By the outbreak of war she was scratching a living as a journalist in London.

She resolved to cover the fighting on the Western Front but was ridiculed by editors unable to secure access for seasoned foreign correspondents.

'I'll see what an ordinary English girl can accomplish,' she wrote. 'I'll see whether I can go one better than these big men with their cars, credentials and money . . . I'll be hanged if I don't try.'

And so she did, befriending the soldiers in Paris – her 'khaki accomplices', as she nicknames them – who would enable her to pass herself off as a Tommy.

Rebecca Nash, curator of the Royal Engineers Museum explains: 'The sappers' uniform would have given Dorothy some leeway to move around – tunnellers had a kind of right to roam. They were not subject to the same military strictures as infantry soldiers, for example, and would often turn up without the commanding officer of an infantry regiment having been informed. It was the perfect cover.'

What was also perfect was meeting Sapper Tommy Dunn on the road to Albert. Beguiled by Dorothy's mad bravery, he resolved to protect her, hiding her in an abandoned cottage until 179 Company troop moved up and she was able to camouflage herself among his comrades. What happened next is open to academic debate. Simon Jones is Britain's foremost expert on the Somme tunnels, and he is not convinced by Dorothy's account. He reveals: 'I am sceptical of the passages in the book in which Dorothy talks of tunnelling under the front line, but there is no doubt whatsoever that she was in the trenches and that she was disguised as a man.'

His conviction is backed by Rebecca Nash. It is further corroborated by letters in the Imperial War Museum archive from Sir Walter Kirke, of the British Expeditionary Force's secret service, which speak of a young female journalist disguised as a man on the front line.

After ten days Dorothy began to suffer fainting fits. She feared that if she were found unconscious her sex would immediately be revealed, compromising Sapper Dunn and others harbouring her.

She gave herself up, only to have a fit of the giggles while being interrogated by the colonel: 'I really could not help it,' she wrote.

'So utterly ludicrous appeared this betrousered little female, marshalled solemnly by three soldiers and deposited before 20 embarrassed men.'

She was sent down the line to Third Army headquarters and subject to a quasi court martial by three generals, who had her locked in a local convent until she could be put on a ferry back across the Channel.

Correspondence held by the Harry Ransom Centre in the University of Texas in Austin includes a letter from Dorothy saying she had had to scrap her first book on the instructions of the War Office, which seems to have invoked the 1914 Defence of the Realm Act to silence her. The letter is on the headed notepaper of The Wide World Magazine, a London-based illustrated monthly where Dorothy appears to have worked.

But even with this journalistic break Dorothy was unable to parlay her experiences and talent into a successful career.

Nor is there any record of her marrying, so when her mental health failed she was incarcerated without argument for the rest of her life.

It's only now, as Britain commemorates the centenary of the Great War, that her unique part in it is being officially recognised with a mention in the new gallery at the Imperial War Museum, which will open this summer.

Curator Laura Clouting said: 'This was a time when there was no provision for women to join any branch of the Services and they weren't even able to work in munitions factories. Mostly they were involved in charity fundraising or succumbed to knitting mania.

'We're including Dorothy Lawrence because she proved the exception to the rule.'

So although she left little trace – no family papers or albums of photographs, and of course, no descendants to celebrate her achievement – 100 years after Dorothy Lawrence became a Sapper on the Somme, her place in history is finally secured

For the Fallen

By Laurence Binyon

With proud thanksgiving, a mother for her children,
England mourns her dead across the sea.
Flesh of her flesh there were, spirit of spirit,
Fallen in the cause of the free.

Solemn the drums thrill: Death august and royal
Sings sorrow up into immortal spheres.
There is music in the midst of desolation
And a glory that shines upon our tears.

They went with songs to the battle, they were young,
Straight of limb, true of eye, steady and aglow.
They were staunch to the end against odds uncounted,
They fell with their faces to the foe.

They shall grow not old, as we that are left grow old;
Age shall not weary them, nor the years condemn.
At the going down of the sun and in the morning
We will remember them.

They mingle not with laughing comrades again;
The sit no more at familiar tables of home;
They haveno lot in our labour of the day-time;
They sleep beyond England's foam.

But where our desires are and our hopes profound,
Felt as a well-spring that is hidden from sight,
To the innermost heart of their own land they are known
As the stars are known to the Night;

As the stars that shall be bright when we are dust,
Moving into marches upon the heavenly plain,
As the stars that are starry in the time of our darkness,
To the end, tto the end, they remain.

For the Fallen was first published in the Times on 21st. September 1914. Laurence Binyon (1869-1943) wrote it while working at the British Museum, and did not go to the Western Front until 1916, as a Red Cross Orderly. The poem's fourth verse is now used all over the world during Services of Remembrance, and is inscribed on countless war monuments.

Recessional

By Rudyard Kipling

God of our fathers, known of old,
Lord of our far-flung battle line,
Beneath whose awful hand we hold
Dominion over palm and pine—
Lord God of Hosts, be with us yet,
Lest we forget—lest we forget!

The tumult and the shouting dies;
The Captains and the Kings depart:
Still stands Thine ancient sacrifice,
An humble and a contrite heart.
Lord God of Hosts, be with us yet,
Lest we forget—lest we forget!

Far-called our navies melt away;
On dune and headland sinks the fire:
Lo, all our pomp of yesterday
Is one with Nineveh and Tyre!
Judge of the Nations, spare us yet,
Lest we forget—lest we forget!

If, drunk with sight of power, we loose
Wild tongues that have not Thee in awe,
Such boastings as the Gentiles use,
Or lesser breeds without the Law—
Lord God of Hosts, be with us yet,
Lest we forget—lest we forget!

For heathen heart that puts her trust
In reeking tube and iron shard,
All valiant dust that builds on dust,
And guarding calls not Thee to guard,
For frantic boast and foolish word—
Thy Mercy on Thy People, Lord!

This is why the phrase **"Lest we forget"** also appears on war monunments.

Part two

Normandy

Normandy tour of 2016
Day One
St Valery en Caux

We visited the monument dedicated to the 51st. Highland Division. It was erected to commemorate the 51st Scottish Division who fought at the Battle of Bréville 8th -13th June 1944, and it is also where Major General Fortune had surrendered to General Rommel in 1940.

Major General Sir Victor Morven Fortune KBE CB DSO DL (21 August 1883 – 2 January 1949) was a senior officer of the British Army. He saw service in both World War I and World War II. He commanded the 51st (Highland) Infantry Division during the Battle of France and was subsequently trapped and obliged to surrender to the Germans on 12 June 1940.

The 51st Division remained in France after the general evacuation from Dunkirk, having been assigned to the French X Corps. After naval evacuation proved impossible and supplies of ammunition had been exhausted, Major-General Fortune was forced to surrender the greater part of the Highland Division at St Valery en Caux. One brigade had earlier withdrawn to Le Havre and avoided capture.

Major General Fortune spent the rest of the war as a prisoner of war. As senior British officer in captivity in Germany, he worked to improve the conditions of the men under his command. He suffered a stroke in 1944 but refused repatriation. He was finally liberated in April 1945 and made KBE shortly after.

The picture on page 91 shows the monument and the harbour that Major General Fortune and his men were heading towards. Sadly, there were no vessels there to take them home to Britain. And so, they surrendered.

Major General Fortune seen here with General Rommel

The Battle of Bréville

The Battle of Bréville was fought by the British 6th Airborne Division and the German 346th Infantry Division, between 8 and 13 June 1944, during the early phases of the invasion of Normandy in the Second World War.

In June 1944, units of the 346th Infantry Division occupied Bréville-les-Monts, a village on a watershed between the rivers Orne and Dives. From this vantage point, they could observe the positions of the 6th Airborne Division, defending the River Orne and Caen Canal bridges and beyond them the British Sword at Ouistreham. Following several German attacks on British positions from Bréville-les-Monts, the capture of the village became essential to secure the 6th Airborne Division positions and protect the Allied beachhead.

The British attack occurred over the night of 12/13 June 1944, when Major-General Richard Nelson Gale committed his only reserves, the 12th (Yorkshire) Parachute Battalion, a company from the 12th Battalion, Devonshire Regiment and the 22nd Independent Parachute Company. To support the attack, a tank squadron from the 13th/18th Royal Hussars and five regiments of artillery were assigned to the division. The assault had to negotiate both the British and German artillery fire, which killed or wounded several men, including some senior officers. The attackers eventually reached and secured the village. However, every officer or sergeant major who took part in the attack was killed or wounded.

After the capture of Bréville, the Germans never seriously attempted to break through the airborne division's lines again. The British division only being subjected to sporadic artillery and mortar fire. This lasted until 17 August, when the Germans started to withdraw and the 6th Airborne Division advanced to the River Seine.

On 6 June 1944, the 6th Airborne Division landed in Normandy to secure the left flank of the British landing zone. The division's objectives were to capture intact the Caen canal bridge, the Orne river bridge, destroy the Merville gun battery – which was in a position to engage troops landing at the nearby Sword – and the bridges crossing the River Dives, the latter to prevent German reinforcements approaching the landings from the east.

The division's two parachute brigades, landing in the early hours of 6 June, were scattered across the countryside during the parachute drop. Most of the battalions could only muster around sixty per cent or less of their total strength on the drop zones (DZ). They did carry out all of their objectives, however, before the 6th

Airlanding Brigade arrived by gliders to reinforce them at 21:00 that evening. The 6th Airborne Division, now with the commandos of the 1st Special Service Brigade under command, had to defend the Orne bridgehead. This was not an easy task as it had to face elements of the 21st Panzer Division from the south and the 346th and 711th Infantry Divisions from the east.

The airborne division's brigades prepared to hold the positions they had captured, with the 5th Parachute Brigade, as the division's depth formation, dug into the east of the River Orne Bridge. The 6th Air landing Brigade was in the south between Longueval and Hérouvillette.

The two remaining brigades dug in along a ridge of high ground that, if lost, offered the Germans a position to look down on the British landing zone. The 1st Special Service Brigade was in the north on a line from Hameau Oger to Le Plain. In between the commandos and the air landing brigade was the 3rd Parachute Brigade.

Their defensive line, however, was incomplete, as the small village of Bréville-les-Monts, between the commandos and the 3rd Parachute Brigade, was held by the Germans. Located on the ridge line it gave the Germans a view into Ranville, at the heart of the British position, the two captured bridges and in the distance Sword.

At 01:30 on 7 June, the 9th Parachute Battalion, with only around ninety men at the time, marched through the unoccupied Bréville. Upon arrival at the 3rd Parachute Brigade's position, the parachute battalion was ordered to dig in at the northern end of the brigade line. They would be responsible for defending an area from the Château Saint Come, across a clearing in the woods, to a house known as the Bois de Mont. To their front was a stretch of open land leading to Bréville-les-Monts and the road from Amfreville to Le Mesnil-les-Monts. A shortage in their numbers left a large gap between the 9th Parachute Battalion and No. 6 Commando, the most southern unit in the commando defensive position, to their north.

By now the German 346th Infantry Division had reached the area from its base at Le Havre. Their first attack, by the 744th Grenadier Regiment, was against the 1st Special Service Brigade. Attacking in strength, they were near to breaking through the line when No. 3 Commando counter-attacked and drove them back.

Later in the morning, No. 6 Commando came under artillery and mortar fire from Bréville. The commandos attacked and cleared the village of Germans, capturing several prisoners, some machine-guns and four artillery pieces. Then they withdrew to their original position. The Germans reoccupied the village and formed their own defensive positions, facing the ridge line defended by the airborne division. Their positions also isolated the 9th Parachute Battalion, which was almost cut off from the rest of the division.

The next day a patrol from the 9th Parachute Battalion reconnoitred the Château Saint Come. They found it abandoned, but the presence of clothing, equipment, a half-eaten meal and a payroll containing 50,000 French francs betrayed the recent German occupancy.

Units of the 857th Grenadier Regiment, part of the 346th Infantry Division, attacked the battalion's position at midday. It appeared to be only a probing attack, easily fought off by 'A' Company. Later the same day the Germans attacked 'A' and 'C' Companies. This time they were repelled by Vickers machine gun fire and a counterattack by the battalion's anti-tank platoon, with a Bren machine gun group under command of the Regimental Sergeant Major.

9 June
Two soldiers of the 6th Airborne Division man a trench beside the Caen road just outside Ranville.

The next German attack was at dawn on 9 June, when a heavy mortar barrage landed on the 9th Parachute Battalion positions. Then 'A' and 'C' Companies were attacked simultaneously. After taking heavy casualties, the Germans retreated into the woods surrounding the Château, where they reformed and attempted another unsuccessful attack an hour later.

Brigade Headquarters was attacked by a force of Germans that had infiltrated through the woods. Informed of the attack, Lieutenant Colonel Terence Otway, the commanding officer of 9th Parachute Battalion, collected 'C' Company, his own headquarters staff and a small group armed with captured German MG 42 machine-guns. They approached the Germans from the rear and trapped them in a crossfire, killing nineteen and capturing one. That afternoon two infantry platoons attacked 'A' Company but were fought off by a counterattack from 'C' Company's position.

At 17:30 a flight of Luftwaffe Focke-Wulf Fw 190s attacked the Orne bridgehead, causing little in the way of any damage. Soon afterward, Royal Air Force Short Stirling bombers arrived to carry out a parachute resupply for the division. Included in the parachute drop were 6 pounder anti-tank guns, which until then had always been delivered by glider. Some forty-one of the 9th

Parachute Battalion's missing men arrived at their position at 21:00, bringing the battalion strength up to around 200 men.

10 June

A reconnaissance patrol from the 13th Parachute Battalion reported a large gathering of Germans in Bréville and suspected an attack was imminent. At 08:00 a massive artillery and mortar bombardment fell along the 1st Special Service Brigade lines, while the 857th Grenadier Regiment, which had gathered in the village, attacked No. 6 Commando. By 10:30, the attack on No. 6 Commando had been driven back, but to their left at Hauger No.4 Commandos had to win a hand-to-hand fight before the Germans withdrew. Twice more during the day the commandos were attacked unsuccessfully, from Sallenelles in the north and again from Bréville.

At 09:00 one battalion of the 857th Grenadier Regiment had crossed the drop zone and approached the 5th Parachute Brigades positions. Its two forward units, the 7th Parachute Battalion and the 13th Parachute Battalion, held their fire until the Germans were only 50 yards (46 m) away. The few survivors of the onslaught escaped into the nearby woods.

Early on 10 June another group of thirty-one men arrived at the 9th Parachute Battalion position. These and other stragglers, who had arrived through the night, brought the battalion strength to around 270 men. At 11:00 the Germans attacked 'A' Company again, but this time the attack was ill-coordinated and was easily repelled. Shortly afterwards the battalion killed around fifty Germans, who had started digging defences in full view of the British position. Then 'A' Company ambushed a German patrol, causing several casualties. That afternoon a strong force of Germans occupied the Château and used it as a base to start an infantry and self-propelled gun assault on the British battalion. With no mortar ammunition left, the British had to use their PIATs and machine-guns to stop the attack.

The next German attack was in force, using the 2nd Battalion 857th Grenadier Regiment, the 1st and 2nd Battalion's 858th Grenadier Regiment and several companies of the 744th Grenadier Regiment with tank and armoured car support. They attempted to force a gap in the British lines between the commandos and the 3rd Parachute Brigade to reach Ranville.

Two infantry companies attacked 'B' Company 9th Parachute Battalion's position. This assault was more determined, even naval gunfire support from the 6-inch (150 mm) guns of HMS Arethusa did not stop the attack. When they reached the British position a hand-to-hand fight ensued, during which most of the Germans were killed. One of the prisoners taken was the commander of the 2nd Battalion 857th Grenadier Regiment, who informed his captors that "his regiment had been destroyed in the fighting against the airborne division". The rest of the German assault came up against the 1st Canadian Parachute Battalion, and was stopped by an artillery bombardment, two later attacks on them suffered the same fate. Later at 23:00 'C' Company 9th Parachute Battalion fought their way to and occupied the Château and fought off several small attacks throughout the night.

With his two parachute brigades and the commando brigade heavily engaged Major General Richard Gale contacted I Corps for armour support. He had decided to clear the woods at Le Mariquet of Germans. The objective was given to the 7th Parachute Battalion and 'B' Squadron 13th/18th Royal Hussars. The tanks would advance over the open ground, their only cover being crashed gliders. Meanwhile, 'A' and 'B' Company's would clear the woods. In the fighting the only British casualties were ten wounded in the parachute battalion, but eight men from the Hussars were killed and four Sherman and two Stuart tanks were destroyed. The Germans from the 857th Grenadier Regiment, had twenty killed and 100 men surrendered, and were driven out of the woods.

The German attacks convinced Lieutenant General John Crocker, commander of 1 Corps, to reinforce the 6th Airborne Division, and the 51st (Highland) Infantry Division was ordered to take over the southern sector of the Orne bridgehead. At the same time the 5th Battalion Black Watch was attached to the 3rd Parachute Brigade. The Black Watch were informed to prepare for an assault to capture Bréville and formed up to the rear of the 9th Parachute Battalion, ready to begin their attack the next day.

11 June

The Black Watch would attack Bréville from the south-west, but before the attack sent a company to take over the defence of the Château. At 04:30 supported by the guns and mortars of the airborne and highland divisions the attack began. To reach Bréville the battalion had to cross 250 yards (230 m) of open ground, and when they neared the village the British artillery ceased fire. The Germans then opened fire with their artillery, mortars and machine-guns. One company was completely wiped out by the German machine-gun fire as it advanced over the open ground. Met with such a heavy concentrated fire, the battalion suffered 200 casualties and the attack was repulsed. The survivors retreated to the Château but were immediately counter-attacked by the 3rd Battalion, 858th Infantry Regiment, who themselves suffered heavy casualties.

That afternoon three troops of tanks from the 13th/18th Royal Hussars, were sent to reinforce the Black Watch, but they had only just started to move towards the

Château when three tanks were destroyed by hidden German self-propelled guns. The other tanks were withdrawn being unable to deploy in the wooded ground around the Château. The rest of the day and night passed without another attack, but the Germans sent out reconnaissance patrols to establish the exact location of the British positions and German armoured vehicles could be heard moving up to the front during the night.

At midday on 12 June the entire 3rd Parachute Brigade position came under artillery and mortar fire prior to a major attack scheduled to start at 15:00. A German battalion attacked the 1st Canadian Parachute Battalion, another supported by six tanks and self-propelled guns attacked the 9th Parachute Battalion and the 5th Black Watch. The battle for the Château cost the Black Watch nine Bren Gun Carriers and destroyed all of their anti-tank guns. Unable to resist they were forced to pull back to the Bois de Mont, joining the 9th Parachute Battalion, which was being attacked by the German armoured vehicles. One tank in front of 'B' Company was hit by two PIAT rounds but remained in action. The tank destroyed two of 'B' company's machine-gun posts, when it was hit by a third anti-tank projectile and withdrew. The attack killed or wounded the last men in the Machine-Gun Platoon and the Anti-Tank Platoon was reduced to one PIAT detachment. The German infantry were in danger of over-running the battalion, when Otway contacted brigade headquarters, informing them they were not able to hold out much longer. Brigadier James Hill personally led a counterattack of forty men from the Canadian battalion which drove off the Germans. By 20:00 the area defended by the two battalions had been cleared of all opposition and the front line restored.

Gale concluded that to relieve the pressure on the division, he had to take Bréville. The only units available for the attack were the division reserve, which consisted of the 12th Parachute Battalion (350 men), and 'D' Company 12th Battalion Devonshire Regiment (eighty-six men). Another unit, the 22nd Independent Parachute Company, the division's pathfinders, were to stand by and respond to any German counterattack. To provide fire support, Gale was given a squadron of tanks from the 13th/18th Royal Hussars, three field artillery regiments armed with 25 pounder guns, a medium artillery regiment of 5.5-inch guns and the division's own artillery the 53rd (Worcester Yeomanry) Airlanding Light Regiment. The attack on Bréville would start at 22:00, timed to catch the Germans tired and off-guard following the days fighting. The start line was on the outskirts of Amfreville, which had already been secured by No.6 Commando.

Lieutenant Colonel Johnny Johnson of the 12th Parachute Battalion was in command of the assault. He decided his own 'C' Company would secure the first crossroads; the Devonshire Company would then clear the north of the village. At the same time 'A' Company would advance through 'C' Company and secure the south-east. At the rear would be 'B' Company the battalion reserve. The attack had to cross 400 yards (370 m) of open ground to reach the village, to support the assault and destroy a German position 200 yards (180 m) from the start line, a troop of Sherman tanks would accompany them.

At 21:50 the British artillery opened fire, and the Germans responded with their own artillery and mortars which forced most of the British to take cover, for the next fifteen minutes, until a lull in the German fire allowed them to continue. In the lead 'C' Company had crossed the start line at 22:00, however all its officers and the company sergeant major (CSM) became casualties and a senior Edmund (Eddie) Warren non-commissioned officer took command of the company. They continued to advance through the artillery and mortar bombardment, guided towards their objective by tracer rounds from the Hussars tanks. Repeatedly hit by the artillery and tanks, Bréville was in flames by the time the company's fifteen survivors reached the village.

The battalion's 'A' Company suffered a similar fate, the officer commanding was wounded crossing the start line, and at the same time every member of the 2nd Platoon was killed or wounded. The Company Sergeant Major assumed command of the company but was killed when they reached Bréville. The company second in command who had been bringing up the rear, reached the village and found the 3rd Platoon only had nine men left but they had managed to clear the village Château and the 1st Platoon had cleared its grounds.

The Devonshire company was moving towards Amfreville when an artillery round landed amongst them wounding several men. As they crossed the start line another shell landed nearby killing Johnson, their company commander Major Bampfylde and wounding Brigadiers Lord Lovat of the commando brigade and Hugh Kindersley of the airlanding brigade, who were observing the attack. Colonel Reginald Parker, deputy commander of the airlanding brigade and a former commanding officer of the 12th Parachute Battalion, had been wounded by the same shell but went forward to take over command of the attack.

By 22:45 the crossroads had been secured by what remained of 'C' Company, the eighteen survivors of 'A' Company were in among the south-eastern buildings of Bréville. In the north-east of the village the twenty survivors of the Devonshire Company had captured their objective. The shelling had stopped when 'B' Company reached the village unopposed and occupied abandoned German trenches beside the church. Fearing a German counterattack on his weakened battalion, Parker ordered a defensive artillery bombardment. However, there was a misunderstanding when the order reached the artillery and a heavy bombardment landed on the British positions in the village, causing several casualties including three of the surviving officers.

At 02:00 on 13 June the 13th/18th Royal Hussars squadron arrived at 'C' Company's position at the crossroads, later followed by fifty-one men from the 22nd Independent Parachute Company. Bréville was now in British control again for the third time since the landings on 6 June. But not in the numbers to defend against a German counterattack, so the 1st Battalion Royal Ulster Rifles, part of the 6th Airlanding Brigade, was moved into the village to take over from the survivors of the attack.

The final attack had cost the 12th Parachute Battalion 126 killed and left its three rifle companies with only thirty-five men between them. The 12th Devonshire Company had another thirty-six killed. Amongst the casualties, were every officer or warrant officer, who had either been killed or wounded. The German defenders from the 3rd Battalion 858th Grenadier Regiment, had numbered 564 men before the British assault, by the time the village had been captured there were only 146 of them left.

However, the left flank of the invasion zone was now secure. On 13 June the 51st (Highland) Infantry Division took over responsibility for the southern sector of the Orne bridgehead, releasing the 6th Airlanding Brigade to strengthen the 6th Airborne Division position along the ridge line. The next two months was a period of static warfare, until 17 August when the division crossed the River Dives and advanced north along the French coast. By the 26 August they had reached Honfleur at the mouth of the River Seine, capturing over 1,000 prisoners and liberating 1,000 square kilometres (390 square miles) of France.

The Battle of Bréville has since been claimed to have been "one of the most important battles of the invasion". Had the division lost the battle, the Germans would have been in a position to attack the landing beaches. But after the battle the Germans never attempted a serious attack on the division again. For their accomplishment, the Battle of Bréville was one of six battle honours awarded to the Parachute Regiment for the Normandy Campaign.

Day Two

Merville Battery

One of the three WW2 veterans to accompany us on this trip was among the first to parachute in with 6th. Airborne to capture Merville Battery, at approximately 00:40 hrs 6th. June 1944.

This young man is George Watt who was part of the 9th. Para who took part in the invasion of Marville Battery, just after midnight on 6th. June 1944. George is seen here inside the actual casement that his platoon captured.

Neutralizing the Merville Battery was the 9th Parachute Battalion's mission in the early hours of D-Day. This amazing site has a command bunker and ten other structures, including four massive casemates that housed 150 mm guns which could have jeopardised the landings on Sword Beach and the Allies eastern flank.

One of the casemates is now a museum which describes in detail the 9th Battalion Parachute Regiment's attack on the Battery. Commanded by Lieutenant Colonel Terence Otway, they had started out with 750 men, but many missed their drop zones and only 150 actually took part in the attack. Of those 65 became casualties, either killed or wounded.

The display is excellent and well presented. There are weapons, uniforms, documents and a film of Lt. Col. Otway telling the story of the attack. If you look up at the roof of the casemates you can see the damage that was done during the attacks.

Lt. Col. Otway was awarded the Distinguished Service Order for his outstanding leadership at Merville Battery and at Le Pein where his depleted force came up against strengthening German resistance. His citation for his DSO reads,

"For conspicuous bravery and outstanding leadership. This officer led 150 men of his battalion on the successful attack on the Sallenelles battery. He personally directed the attack and organised the successful cleaning up of the enemy strong points under heavy enemy mortar and machine gun fire. He led the attack on and successfully held Le Pein until relieved by another formation. On arrival in the Le Mesnil area he succeeded in beating off two major enemy attacks of several hours' duration by his magnificent of his numerically very weak tired battalion. His utter disregard of personal danger has been an inspiration for all his men."

There is also an educational trail with information boards with photographs and text detailing how a German artillery battery worked, the position of the battery in Hitler's Atlantic Wall, how it was constructed, and the daily routine of the soldiers.

One bunker recreates the attack on Merville Battery with sound, light, smoke and odours combining in s deluge of noise and fire. The noise is so loud that there are notices warning people before entering.

Also, on site is a USAAF Douglas C-47 transport plane which took part in the Normandy landings. Information boards tell the story of what happened to it after the war and how it was recovered and restored.

There are numerous plaques and memorials throughout the site including a bronze bust of Lt. Col. Otway which was unveiled by him in 1997.

This picture shows Lt. Col. Terence Otway Officer Commanding 9th. Parachute Battalion bronze bust which he unveiled in 1997.

One of the signs for the Educational trail at Batterie de Merville

Another sign for the educational trail at Batterie de Merville

Ranville War Cemetery

Ranville was the first village to be liberated in France when the bridge over the Caen Canal was captured intact in the early hours of 6th June by the troops of the 6th. Airborne Division. Many of their casualties are buried here in the Ranville War Cemetery.

Private Emile Corteil, a 19-year-old dog handler with the 9th. Battalion Parachute Regiment jumped with his dog "Glen" on the early hours of D-Day. He was part of the mission to secure the flanks of the landings and knock out the Merville Battery which imposed a threat to the British landing beaches.

Like so many jumps that night, he missed his night-time landing zone. He was linking up with the rest of 9 Para to attack the Merville Battery when they were hit by RAF friendly fire, killing or wounding the majority of the 60 paratroopers assembled. Both Emile and Glen were killed. Only 150 of the original 750 got to their rendezvous point and only 85 survived the attack on Merville Battery.

Because Emile and Glen were so close and devoted to each other in life, they were no to be separated in death and Glen is the only animal believed to be buried in a Commonwealth War Grave. Emile's epitaph reads, *"Had you known our boy you would have loved him too. 'Glen,' his paratroop dog was killed with him"*.

Another young soldier buried here is a 16-year-old believed to be the youngest British Soldier to die during the war. Private Robert Johns, from Portsmouth, was shot dead as A Company 13th. Parachute Battalion, part of the 3rd. Airborne Brigade, defended Le Msnil crossroads. He was a very big built lad and it was only when he died did it come to light that he was only 14 years old when he joined the regiment.

There are two Canadian brothers buried side by side. Lieutenant J. Phillippe Rousseau, 1st. Canadian Parachute Battalion, killed 7th. June 1944, and Lieutenant Joseph Maurice Rousseau, 1st. Canadian Parachute Battalion, killed 20th. September 1944.

There are also several members of 2nd. Royal Ulster Rifles, friends of Scottish War Blinded member, Hugh McGuire are buried here.

Hugh McGuire, was a member of the 2nd. Bn. Royal Ulster Rifles, who had landed on Sword Beach, 6th. June 1944, on page 103 there is a short recollection of what the Battalion did after getting off Sword Beach and their push into the City of Caen.

Men of the 2nd Battalion of the Royal Ulster Rifles with General Montgomery

2nd Royal Ulster Rifles
Entering Caen

The Battalion first heard that it was to have the honour of leading the Allied Armies into Caen on the afternoon of 7th July 1944. After three weeks in the line at Cambes, we had been pulled out for a rest at St Aubin d'Arquenay, but had only been there for a single day when we were ordered to move forward again to positions behind 185 Brigade at Bieville prior to passing through them into Caen.

The plan was as follows: 185 Brigade was to capture Lebisey Wood, and, having consolidated, to seize the high ground above Caen on Ring Contour 60. The 2nd Battalion the Royal Ulster Rifles, supported by 1st Battalion The King's Own Scottish Borderers, was to move up to the heights and, from there, thrust down into Caen. The first half of this plan consisted of a deliberate attack, based upon information about the strength and dispositions of the enemy which had been accumulated since D Day. The second half, in which the Battalion was to be committed, depended entirely upon the progress and success of the first. Our task was to maintain the momentum of the first assault and to pursue the enemy to the far side of the river Orne.

185 Brigade launched their attack at 0400 hours 8th July. Shortly afterwards, our own Brigade moved forward into the positions from which 185 had gone forward. It was a clear night with a full moon, and as we moved forward, we could see the flashes and hear the rumble of the tremendous barrage which pounded the enemy for some hours before zero. By dawn, we were secure in Bieville, providing a firm base for the 185 attack.

By 1000 hours the objective Lebisey Wood was reported taken; but mopping up and consolidation took time and not until 1500 hours did the reserve battalion of 185 Brigade, the 2nd K. S. L. I., begin the advance towards Ring Contour 60. Meanwhile the Commanding Officer was making his reconnaissance and evolving a plan with the Commander of the supporting tank unit, the 1st Northants Yeomanry, assisted by Major W. D. Tighe-Wood and Captain A. C. Bird, commanding the two forward companies. At 1430 hours the Battalion moved forward and debouched from Lebisey Wood towards Ring Contour 60 at 1730 hours.

At this time no news of the progress of the K. S. L. I. had reached us, nor had we heard anything of enemy dispositions behind Lebisey Wood.

However, it was obvious from the viewpoint of Lebisey that the Boche was shelling intensively the whole area between the wood and Ring Contour 60, by using as O. Ps the chimneys of the factories at Colombelles lying on the south side of the Orne to the N. E. of Caen. These chimneys constituted too small a target for the RAF or for our own gunners, yet they dominated the battlefield, and made the passage of our troops a difficult one.

'A' and 'D' Companies, however, moved forward according to plan. At first, while they were operating in close touch with the tanks, the enemy barrage was not troublesome; but later the range was closed, and some damage was done. 'A' Company had just established itself on the objective when Company Headquarters received a direct hit which wounded Major W. D. Tighe-Wood and a number of his staff. Captain C. G. Alexander took over command. Meanwhile liaison had been made with the K. S. L. I. and with supporting tanks providing admirable cover and protection against a counterattack, everyone dug in with the utmost rapidity. Little small arms fire had been met and prisoners were few, but the position was being continuously and accurately shelled. 'A' Company again suffered; this time its Stretcher Bearers "were all wounded, and great work was done by Cpl Reid, Rfn A. Cranston and Rfn Devaney in bringing in and tending the wounded, 'B' and 'C', the two reserve companies, who moved up to the position under heavy shellfire also suffered casualties.

By the time the whole Battalion was in position, it was getting late and the light was beginning to fail. We had about 80 casualties, mostly from shellfire, since such Germans as had been found on the objective were swiftly liquidated. Nevertheless, we were determined to make an effort to enter Caen that evening, and 'B' Company under Major J. W. Hyde, with two troops of tanks, set off to probe the enemy positions in the Northern approaches to the town. Some casualties on the start line were caused by an 88 mm gun, and opposition was encountered some 500 yards further on. The tanks were completely held up by the havoc and ruin wrought in bombing attacks by the RAF and our men themselves could only move forward with the utmost difficulty. Finally, mines were discovered on the track and its verges. It was considered unwise to continue this operation by night, and so 'B' Company, under orders from the Commanding Officer, returned to their original positions.

Early next morning, two more patrols were sent out. One platoon of 'A' Company, under Lt R. Wise "with a troop of tanks went down to Calix on the Eastern outskirts of Caen and, simultaneously, another platoon, also 'A' Company, under Lt B. R. Burges moved to Lt Julien in the North West of the town. The first patrol reached its objective and remained there until recalled later in the day. It had trouble with snipers and the Platoon Commander was himself wounded in the head. Lt Burges with his platoon reached Lt Julien, and then began an advance of his own accord into the heart of the town. Some light resistance was brushed aside but later on the defences stiffened and casualties were sustained. Lt Burges was himself wounded, though able to retain control of his platoon, and two of his N. C. Os, were killed outright. Thereupon this patrol returned to its position at St Julien and did not link up again with the Battalion until the following day. It may be said, however, that this platoon was the first into the heart of the town because the Canadians did not appear on the right until late in the afternoon and the forward elements of our own Battalion were not in Caen much before 1100 hours.

At 0930 hours 9th July the Battalion began their advance into Caen. 'B' Company led the way progressing slowly but surely, systematically clearing the ruins of enemy. Small groups of retreating Germans were dealt with, but no organised opposition was met, and abandoned machine gun posts and rocket apparatus testified to the swiftness of his withdrawal. Owing to the rubble and devastation caused by the bombing, movement was slow and difficult. There was no question of vehicle movement here, and so throughout this advance the infantry relied solely and entirely upon their own resources.

By 1130 hours Major Hyde was astride the Boulevardes des Allies and the remainder of the Battalion was pressing forward. Some casualties were sustained by 'D' Company before moving off from Hill 60, where Lt Palmer and his Platoon Sergeant were both wounded and evacuated: but L/Sgt Bonass assumed command and led the Platoon calmly and efficiently for the rest of the action.

When the main body of the Battalion reached down into the town, the advance soon assumed the air of triumphant progress rather than a calculated operation of war; the people of Caen were determined to make it so. We discovered afterwards that they had suffered all the brutalities that had become commonplace in Europe. In addition, they had seen their town laid waste in a series of RAF attacks, by their own friends, the British. If we were ever doubtful of a welcome reception, the first few hours in Caen put our minds at rest. Flags of Fighting France were draped out of windows, and the people poured out of their houses with greetings and glasses of wine.

On the Boulevardes we were met by the Captain of the Resistance Movement with several of his comrades who gave us "Liberte" as the password agreed upon by themselves and their Headquarters in London. One of their number guided 'C' Company along the Boulevardes and others proved themselves invaluable in disclosing hide-outs of German snipers and machine gunners. It may be said here that through the complete mastery of the language displayed by Major J. C. S. G. de Longueuil we were able to take full advantage of their assistance.

We met many other interesting people in Caen, two of whom may be mentioned here. One was Squadron Leader Sprawson, DFC, RAF whose Lancaster had been shot down near Caen on D Day and who had since then been sheltering with a patriot family in Caen itself. Having experienced RAF bombing at the receiving end, he was anxious to get back, and having paused for a brief moment at Brigade Headquarters to make a recording for the BBC, he hurried back to England. The second was a Frenchman "whom our men found to be widely travelled but who reached the peak of his popularity when he revealed himself to be a regular of "Mooneys" in Belfast. Needless to say, he was an old soldier.

The rest of the operation can be swiftly summarised. We pushed gradually down to the line of the River Orne and then systematically mopped up such disorganised resistance as remained. Our most lasting impression and remembrance of Caen will be the magnificent spirit of friendship and co-operation displayed by its citizens. The men of The Royal Ulster Rifles will pay them lasting tribute and can hope to have done something towards forging a bond of mutual sympathy and friendship.

The Ranville War Cemetery contains 2235 Commonwealth graves from World War II, sadly 97 of them have never been identified. The cemetery also has 330 German graves and some of other nationalities.

2nd Battalion Royal Ulster Rifles in Normandy

Company Quartermaster Sergeant WJ Sharkey receiving the
Distinguished Conduct Medal from General Montgomery

Pegasus Bridge

In the movie "The Longest Day" actor Richard Todd played the part of Major John Howard; whose instructions were to *"hold the bridge until relieved."*

The picture above is the original bridge from the D Day landings. The bridge is no longer in use and has been moved to a new permanent location near the Pegasus Memorial Museum as seen in the picture on the next page.

This picture shows from a Horsa glider as used during the actual invasion.

The Picture above shows a memorial to Brigadier James Hill.

Brigadier Stanley James Ledger Hill, DSO & Two Bars, MC served as commander of the 3rd Parachute Brigade, part of the 6th Airborne Division, during the Second World War. Born in Bath, Somerset, Hill was educated at Marlborough College and the Royal Military College, Sandhurst. After a brief period of time in the Irish Free State, he volunteered for parachute training and joined the 1st Parachute Battalion, and was its commanding officer when its parent formation, the 1st Parachute Brigade, was deployed to North Africa.

The Battle for Pegasus Bridge

On the night of 5 June 1944, a force of 181 men, led by Major John Howard, took off from RAF Tarrant Rushton in Dorset, southern England in six Horsa gliders to capture Pegasus Bridge, and also "Horsa Bridge", a few hundred yards to the east, over the Orne River. The force was composed of D Company (reinforced with two platoons of B Company), 2nd Battalion, Oxford and Bucks Light Infantry; 20 sappers of the Royal Engineers of 249 Field Company (Airborne); and men of the Glider Pilot Regiment. The object of this action was to prevent German armour from crossing the bridges and attacking the eastern flank of the landings at Sword Beach.

Five of the Ox and Bucks's gliders landed as close as 47 yards from their objectives from 16 minutes past midnight. The attackers poured out of their battered gliders, completely surprising the German defenders, and took the bridges within 10 minutes. They lost two men in the process, Lieutenant Den Brotheridge and Lance corporal Fred Greenhalgh.

Greenhalgh drowned in a nearby pond when his glider landed. Lieutenant Brotheridge was mortally wounded crossing the bridge in the first minutes of the assault and became the first member of the invading Allied armies to die as a result of enemy fire on D-Day.

One glider, assigned to the capture of the river bridge, landed at the bridge over the River Dives, some 7 miles off. Most of the soldiers in this glider moved through German lines towards the village of Ranville where they eventually re-joined the British forces. The Ox and Bucks were reinforced at 03.00 hrs by Lieutenant Colonel Pine-Coffin's 7th Parachute Battalion and linked up with the beach landing forces with the arrival of Lord Lovat's 6 Commando of the 1st. Special Service Brigade, including Piper Bill Millen.

One of the members of the 7th Battalion reinforcements was Captain Richard Todd, a young actor, who would, as I mentioned at the start of this section, nearly two decades later, play Major Howard in the film The Longest Day. The photo above shows Peter Lawford (left, portraying Lord Lovatt,) and Richard Todd, (centre, portraying Major John Howard.)

The bridge was renamed "Pegasus" Bridge as a tribute the British Airborne whose insignia was the "Pegasus" the Winged Horse, which was chosen by Daphne du Maurier, the author, the wife of General Sir Frederick Browning, the war time commander of Airborne Forces.

Juno Beach Museum

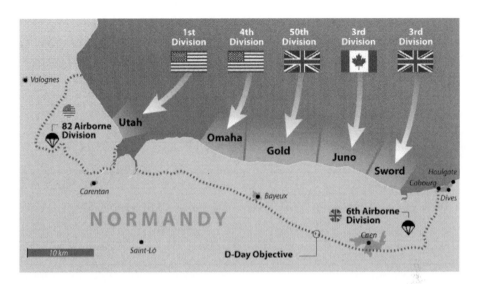

As you can see from the map above Juno beach was a predominantly Canadian affair. In particular the 3rd Infantry Division, the 2nd. Armoured Brigade and from Britain, 48 Royal Marine Commandos.

Many of you may recognise the Officer above. He became famous for his portrayal of Commander Scott on the USS Enterprise, in the TV show "Star Trek." Lt. James Doohan joined the Royal Canadian Artillery and was a member of the 14th (Midland) Field Battery, 2nd Canadian Infantry Division. He was commissioned a lieutenant in the 14th Field Artillery Regiment of the 3rd Canadian Infantry Division. He was sent to England in 1940 for training. He first saw combat landing at Juno Beach on D-Day.

Shooting two snipers, Doohan led his men to higher ground through a field of anti-tank mines, where they took defensive positions for the night. Crossing between command posts at 11:30 that night, Doohan was hit by six rounds fired from a Bren gun by a nervous Canadian sentry: four in his leg, one in the chest, and one through his right middle finger. The bullet to his chest was stopped by a silver cigarette case given to him by his brother. His right middle finger had to be amputated, something he would conceal on-screen during most of his career as an actor.

Doohan graduated from Air Observation Pilot Course 40 with eleven other Canadian artillery officers and flew Taylorcraft Auster Mark V aircraft for 666 (AOP) Squadron, RCAF as a Royal Canadian Artillery officer in support of 1st Army Group Royal Artillery. All three Canadian (AOP) RCAF squadrons were manned by artillery officer-pilots and accompanied by non-commissioned RCA and RCAF personnel serving as observers.

Although he was never actually a member of the Royal Canadian Air Force, Doohan was once labelled the "craziest pilot in the Canadian Air Force". In the late spring of 1945, on Salisbury Plain north of RAF Andover, he slalomed a plane between telegraph poles "to prove it could be done", earning himself a serious reprimand. (Various accounts cite the plane as a Hurricane or a jet trainer; however, it was a Mark IV Auster.) Doohan received many decorations for his military service. These include being made a Lieutenant of the Royal Victorian Order. This is usually awarded for personal service to the Sovereign.

Before we departed from Juno Beach to return to our hotel, we were all invited to take a small reseal able sandwich bag, and to go down onto the beach and to fill our bags with sand from the Normandy beach.

This monument stands on the seaward side of the Museum.

Juno Beach was the designated landing beach for the 3rd. Canadian Infantry Division commanded by General Kellar. It stretched from Ver-sur-Mer to Saint-Aubin-sur-Mer.

The German defences had included fortifying the mouth of the river Seulles in Courseulles-sur-Mer. At 07:45 hrs on D-Day the amphibious tanks of the 1st. Hussars were launched 3 kilometers from the coast. Unfortunately, most of them sank because of heavy seas. Those that succeeded in reaching the beach immediately opened fire on the German positions and enabled the 7th. Brigade to advance quickly inland. Courseulles-sur-Mer was liberated in a few hours. By the evening of 6th. June, 21,500 men and 3,200 vehicles had already landed on Juno Beach.

Day Three

Longues Sur Mer Gun Battery

Longues Sur Mer Gun Battery appears in the movie The Longest Day quite often in the early half of the movie.

This picture shows my son on the left standing on top of one of these Gun emplacements that faced out across from Normandy to Britain.

This was the view looking out to sea from on top of the gun emplacement.

This picture shows the view from inside one of the gun emplacements, this gun emplacement is the actual one used in the movie The Longest Day when the German Officer, **Major Werner Pluskat**, whilst speaking on the phone to **Lt. Col. Oker**, says:

"You know those five thousand ships you say the Allies haven't got? Well, they've got them!"

Lt. Col. Ocker: And just where, my dear Pluskat, are those ships going?

Maj. Werner Pluskat: Straight for me!

This gun emplacement took a direct hit from one of the naval vessels in the Chanel bombarding the Normandy coast ahead of the main invasion.

Two further gun emplacements showing the damage caused by the naval bombardment.

The Longues-sur-Mer Battery (also known as Batterie Allemande) was part of Hitlers Atlantic Wall defences consisting of four rapid firing 152mm navy guns, each housed in large concrete casemates. The site of the battery also included a fire control post, ammunition stores, defensive machine gun posts and accommodation for the soldiers.

The battery is located between Omaha and Gold beach which made it a threat to the Allied landings. Because of this, the area was heavily bombed on the night before D-Day. This was followed by a naval bombardment in the morning. Although the bombing did not cause much damage to the guns it did destroy the phone line linking the fire control bunker to the guns which severely disrupted the batteries ability to engage with the Allied ships that eventually knocked the guns out of action during a duel in which no Allied ship was damaged despite the battery firing 170 rounds. On the 7th of June the major responsible for the battery surrendered to the British with 184 men.

The battery at Longues-sur-Mer was situated between the landing beaches Omaha and Gold. In the build-up to D-Day, the battery was attacked by aircraft on several occasions. On the evening of 5/6 June 1944 the battery was attacked by bombers, but little damage was inflicted on the casemates, but bombs severed the armoured communication system. A large amount of the bombs dropped hit a nearby village. The fire control post reverted to visual signals to control some of the guns and this affected their accuracy.

The bombing was followed from 05:37 on the morning of the landings by bombardment from the British cruiser HMS Ajax. The battery itself opened fire at 06:05, and at 06.20 targeted the headquarters ship for Gold Beach, HMS Bulolo, which retreated out of range.

At 08.00 the British cruisers Ajax and Argonaut engaged the battery. By 08.45 no further shots were fired by the battery's guns for a time as the Germans undertook repairs. The heaviest damage was caused by the explosion of the ammunition for an AA gun, mounted by the Germans on the roof of casemate No.4, which killed several German soldiers.

After effecting repairs the battery's guns once again opened fire towards Omaha Beach. The French cruisers Georges Leygues and Montcalm, assisted by the cruiser U.S.S. Arkansas returned fire on the battery. The return fire knocked out one casemate and damaged two others. The still active fourth gun opened fire intermittently during the afternoon and evening of D-Day but caused little impact on the Allied landings. The battery had fired over 100 shots through the day.

The crew of the battery (184 men, half of them over 40 years old) surrendered without a fight to advancing British troops of Company C of the 2nd Devonshire Regiment at midday on June 7.

Arromanche D-Day Museum

And

Mulberry Harbour

This museum which opened on 5th. Jun 1954 was the first museum to be built in commemoration of the Normandy landings and the Normandy Campaign. It uses an excellent model of the Mulberry Harbour to explain the formidable challenge it took to build in Britain, tow it over the Channel and re-assemble off the coast. The museum overlooks the site where Mulberry B was constructed and most of it can still be seen just a few hundred metres away.

If you look closely the thin black lines on the horizon are remnants of the Mulberry B harbour parts have sunk whilst others are still seen in the harbour.

After the disastrous landing attempt at Dieppe in August 1942, where horrendous losses were sustained, it made the Allies realise that the ports in the English

Channel were too heavily fortified to capture. They had to find another way to land an invasion and have it properly supplied.

Even before the Dieppe raid, Winston Churchill was trying to get a solution which would be an alternative to capturing a port in which to supply ground troops. He sent a very famous memo to Lord Louis Mountbatten about constructing a floating pier head: "They float up and down with the tide. The anchor problem must be mastered. Let me have the best solution."

On D-Day, 6th. June 1944, there were over 4,000 allied ships which successfully achieved the greatest landings in history, and they took the Germans completely by surprise. Now they needed to move men and materials ashore.

Our two D-Day Veterans, Hugh McGuire and George Watt, were each presented with these Commemorative medals (seen here in the actual size) by the Museum Management. George Brown was ill so did not make the trip on this occasion, but a Scottish War Blinded member of staff collected George's medal for him. Hugh was also invited to sign the museums Special Visitors Book.

This picture shows the front of the Commemorative medals

There would be two artificial harbours (Mulberry A at Omaha and Mulberry B at Arromanche). They would comprise of floating roadways and pier heads. In Order to shelter them from the heavy seas, huge hollow reinforced concrete blocks, called Phoenix caissons, and old ships were sunk to create breakwaters. This was a tremendous feat of engineering and took less than nine months to complete in Britain, despite a war industry that were overstretched.

The first ships were scuttled on 7th. June and the next day saw the first submersion of the first Phoenix caissons. The first supplies were unloaded on 14th. June at Mulberry B, now named Port Winston. This amazing feat of engineering was the vital key to providing victory in Europe. At Mulberry B they were unloading more than 18,000 tonnes of supplies on some days.

As well as telling the incredible story of the Mulberry Harbours, the museum also features more than 2,000 different items. There are scale models extending 30 metres, a diorama and archive footage which shows the tremendous effort in the invasion launched by the Allies. There are brochures available in 18 different languages, the diorama in in 6 languages and the archive film is available in 9 languages.

The picture above shows the entrance to the Arromanche Museum

This wall painting was spotted not far from the museum, prompting the question, "Has Banksy been here?"

Colleville-sur-Mer American Cemetery

The Normandy American Cemetery and Memorial in France is located in Colleville-sur-Mer, on the site of the temporary American St. Laurent Cemetery, established by the U.S. First Army on June 8, 1944 as the first American cemetery on European soil in World War II. The cemetery site, at the north end of its half mile access road, covers 172.5 acres and contains the graves of 9,387 of our military dead, most of whom lost their lives in the D-Day landings and ensuing operations. On the Walls of the Missing, in a semi-circular garden on the east side of the memorial, are inscribed 1,557 names. Rosettes mark the names of those since recovered and identified.

The memorial consists of a semi-circular colonnade with a loggia at each end containing large maps and narratives of the military operations; at the centre is the bronze statue, "Spirit of American Youth Rising from the Waves." An orientation table overlooking the beach depicts the landings in Normandy. Facing west at the memorial, one sees in the foreground the reflecting pool; beyond is the burial area with a circular chapel and, at the far end, granite statues representing the United States and France.

The picture above is the only graves marked off with cords, they are the graves of Lt. Quentin Roosevelt who died 18th. July 1918 and Brigadier Theodore Roosevelt Jr. who died of a heart attack 12th. July 1944. Teddy junior's details on his cross are in gold because he was a Medal of Honour recipient.

Their graves a cordoned off because they are son of Teddy Roosevelt the 26th. President of the United States of America.

The picture below shows the view of the English Channel from the top of the cliffs above Omaha Beach.

There is an orientation table which overlooks the beach and depicts the landings at Normandy. Facing west at the memorial, there is a reflecting pool, with the mall with burial areas to both side, and the circular chapel beyond.

The Chapel's mosaic ceiling depicts America blessing her sons as they depart by the sea and air, and a grateful France bestowing a laurel wreath upon the American dead.

On 8th June 1944 the Americans established a temporary cemetery at St. Laurent Cemetery. It was the first time that the Americans created a cemetery on European soil in World War II. It is now one of fourteen World War II Military Cemeteries on foreign soil.

The Roosevelt brothers are among some 33 sets of brothers who have been buried side by side in this one cemetery. There are many other brothers who have not been buried side by side here.

Brigadier General Theodore Roosevelt Jr. Medal of Honour winner.

The pictures below show, Matt Damen and the real-life soldier that he portrayed in the Spielberg / Hanks movie "Saving Private Ryan." Except the soldier on the left of these two photos is called Frederick "Fritz" Niland.

The pictures above show, Matt Damen and the real-life soldier he portrayed in the Spielberg / Hanks movie "Saving Private Ryan." Except that the soldier on the left of these two photos is called Frederick "Fritz" Niland.

Tom Hanks decided to change the name of the movie to give the family some privacy. The name Ryan was chosen as there are more Ryan's buried here than any other name.

Father Sampson Army Chaplain whose part in
Saving Private Ryan was played by Tom Hanks.

Technical Sergeant Edward Niland (December 22, 1912 – February 1984), U.S. Army Air Forces: Imprisoned in a Japanese POW camp in Burma, he was captured on May 16, 1944, and liberated on May 4, 1945.Edward had parachuted from his B-25 Mitchell and wandered the jungles of Burma before being captured. He was held as a prisoner for a year before being liberated in May 1945. Edward lived in Tonawanda until his death in 1984 at the age of 71. In D-Day June 6, 1944, Ambrose incorrectly states that Edward died in Burma.

Second Lieutenant Preston Niland (1915–June 7, 1944), 29, 22nd Infantry Regiment, 4th Infantry Division, was killed in action on June 7, 1944, in Normandy, near Utah Beach.

Technical Sergeant Robert "Bob" Niland (1919–June 6, 1944), 25, D Company, 505th Parachute Infantry Regiment, 82nd Airborne Division was killed in action on June 6, 1944 in Normandy. He volunteered to stay behind with two other men and hold off a German advance while his company retreated from Neuville-au-Plain. He was killed while manning his machine gun; the other two men survived.

Sergeant Frederick "Fritz" Niland (April 23, 1920 – December 1, 1983), H Company, 501st Parachute Infantry Regiment, part of the 101st. Airborne Division: Fritz was close friends with Warren Muck and Donald Malarkey, from E Company, 506th Parachute Infantry Regiment, 101st Airborne Division. Fritz fought through the first few days of the Normandy campaign. Several days following D-Day, Fritz had gone to the 82nd Airborne Division to see his brother, Bob. Once he arrived at division, he was informed that Bob had been killed on D-Day. Fritz was shipped back to England, and finally, to the U.S., where he served as an MP in New York until the completion of the war. Fritz was awarded a Bronze Star for his service. This story is evidenced in Stephen Ambrose's book Band of Brothers, as well as from biographical data on Sampson. Private James Ryan in the film Saving Private Ryan is loosely based on him. Fritz died in 1983 in San Francisco at the age of 63.

Point de Hoc

This picture taken by my eldest son AJ, shows the reverse view to the one that the men from Colonel Rudder's 2nd Rangers Battalion when they were storming the cliff face.

The events surrounding the actual assault on Pointe du Hoc, were not as simple as we saw in the movie The Longest Day. In the movie the assault appeared to be relatively easy. But in reality, this was not the case.

Point du Hoc was a strategic objective in the sector of Omaha Beach. The Germans had built a major coastal battery that could threaten the landing beaches. The range of these 155 mm artillery guns was 15 miles and that could take out ships and hit both the beaches of Utah and Omaha. It was a major objective and key defensive strongpoint which had to be taken out.

On 6th. June 1944 at 05:45 hrs, Colonel Rudder's 2nd. Rangers Battalion of 225 men transferred into the landing ships. They were in the landing craft for more than three hours. It was wet and windy with waves often between three to six feet high. Three assault craft out of the twelve transporting the Rangers Battalion sank before they had reached the beach.

Inscription on the Monument to Colonel Rudder's 2nd. Rangers Battalion, at Point du Hoc.

The Germans thought the cliffs were unassailable from the beach, but the Rangers had been practising with grapnel hooks fired from mortar tubes to get up the 150-foot-high cliffs. However, on D-Day, there were 60 ropes that were soaked through with sea water, only 19 ropes were dry and only 3 ropes reached the top.

However, with fitted ladders and grabs the Rangers climbed the cliff under German machine-gun fire. Resistance was fierce from the Germans. Once at the top they discovered a lunar landscape, but there were no 155 mm guns, only telegraph poles. They suffered 20 casualties.

133

They gradually moved inland, and two Rangers spotted the well camouflaged 155 mm guns sitting mysteriously silent. They destroyed the guns with thermite grenades.

The Germans launched counter attacks and in the evening of 7th. June, after fierce fighting, only 90 men out of Colonel Rudder's battalion were still able to fight. They were relieved on 8th. June by the 29th. Infantry Division arriving from the east. 80 Rangers had been killed.

The Monument in memory of the 2nd. Rangers Battalion on Point du Hoc, is built on a control firing casemate where bodies of the soldiers still lie under the ruins. It is a simple granite pylon and it was transferred to the American Battle Monuments Commission for perpetual care and maintenance on 11th. January 1979.

Point du Hoc is one of the rare locations which portray the violence of the landings. This battle-scarred area on the left flank of Omaha Beach remains just as the Rangers left it.

The Command Post has recently been opened after months of work to consolidate the cliff. There is a plaque which commemorates the fallen from the battle of Pointe du Hoc.

2nd. Rangers climbing to the summit of Point du Hoc

135

Our final day

Le Cambe en Plein Cemetery

There are several Regiments that have fallen comrades in this cemetery, as can be seen by the various Regimental crest on the headstones.

A unit of the East Riding Yeomanry, R. A. C., in support of the 3rd. British Infantry Division, reached the northern outskirts of Cambes-en Plein on 9th. June. Here they found Germans dug in and the advance to Caen was halted.

The original burials date from 8-12 July 1944, when the final attack on Caen (Operation Charnwood) was in progress. By noon on 9th. July most of Caen, north of the river Orne had been captured.

More than half of the graves here belong to the 59th. (Staffordshire) Division, in particular units of the South Staffordshire Regiment, which was involved in this battle. In total there are 224 World War II soldiers buried here.

Time to head off home.

24 little known facts about D-Day

1. To plan for the Operation the BBC ran a competition for French beach holiday photographs. It was actually a way of gathering intelligence on suitable beaches.

2. D-Day is simply a standard armed forces way of emphasising a particular day. It means **THE DAY**. It's like saying H-hour which is the exact time at which an attack traditionally began.

3. From 12th. March 1944 Britain barred all travel to Ireland in order to prevent the leaking of the date of the D-Day landings.

4. The planners were particular about the timing of D-Day. They wanted a full moon, with a spring tide. They wanted to land at dawn on a flood tide, when it was about halfway in. That meant there were only a few days that were appropriate. 5th. June was chosen but it had to be delayed 24 hours because of bad weather conditions.

5. The weather forecast was so bad that the German Commander in Normandy, Erwin Rommel, went home to give his wife a pair shoes on her birthday. He was in Germany when the news of the invasion came in.

6. Lord Lovat landed on Sword Beach with his Commando Brigade, accompanied by his bagpiper, Glasgow-born, Bill Millen. Millen struck up 'Heiland Laddie' as soon as he jumped into the shallows and then walked up and down the beach playing his bagpipes. German prisoners later admitted that they had not attempted to shoot him because they thought he had lost his mind. Bill Millen's bagpipes are now on display in the Pegasus Museum.

7. Hungarian-born photographer Robert Cappa, working for Life Magazine, was the first photographer to land on Omaha Beach, on one the earliest waves. He took over 100 photographs, but an over excited darkroom assistant in London melted the majority of them during development. Only 11 were salvaged. Life printed them and said that they were blurry because Cappa's hands were shaking with the heightened drama of the moment.

8. Before D-Day mini subs crept into the beaches and by night engineers would swim out to take soil samples, then swim back, sleep submerged all day in the subs, then repeat the following evening.

9. The British Infantryman was paid £3 15 shillings per month, whereas the Americans got £12 per month.

10. British Intelligence had set up a network of fake agents who fed the Germans misinformation. The Germans paid good money, meaning that they were paying into the British Exchequer. A useful contribution to the war effort.

11. It was the biggest seaborne invasion in history: 7,000 ships took part.

12. On the night of the invasion only 15% of paratroopers landed in the right place.

13. The German air force, the Luftwaffe, was outnumbered 30:1 on D-Day and didn't shoot down a single allied plane in air to air combat.

14. The first allied soldier killed was Lieutenant Herbert Denham "Den" Brotheridge, just after midnight on the 6th. June, while leading a charge to seize Pegasus Bridge.

15. The most exotic German prisoner captured by the allies in Normandy was Yang Kyoungjong. He was a Korean that had been captured at 18 years of age by the Japanese Army in 1938. He was then captured by the Russians after a Japanese military incursion in 1939. The Russians made him fight the Germans when they were invaded, and he was captured and conscripted in turn by the Germans in 1943. Finally, he was captured by the Americans on D-Day. He then moved to Illinois, where he died in 1992.

16. Prime Minister Winston Churchill announced that he intended to go to sea with the fleet and watch the D-Day landings from HMS Belfast. This idea was opposed by many and it took King George VI to stop him, by insisting that if Churchill went, he would also go. Eventually that made Churchill back down.

17. Commonwealth personnel, nearly all British and Canadian, outnumbered the Americans on D-Day. Of the 156,000 men landed in France on 6th.

June 1944, 73,000 were Americans, and 83,000 were British and Canadian, while the naval contingent was twice that of the Americans.

18. There were five beaches, codenamed from east to west, Sword, Juno, Gold, Omaha and Utah. Casualties varied widely. On 'Bloody Omaha' where around 4,000 men were killed or injured. One American unit landing in the first wave, lost 90% of its men. On Gold Beach, by contrast, casualty rates were around 80% lower.

19. The allies put a huge effort into persuading the Germans that the invasion was going to be around Calais, not Normandy. They invented a whole group of armies in Kent, building dummy equipment and placing General George Patton, who the Germans considered the best allied general, in South East England. The Germans took the bait so much that even after D-Day they held many of their best troops in the Calais area expecting a second invasion.

20. The S. A. S. masterminded parachute drops in which hundreds of dummies were thrown out of aircraft to confuse the Germans as to where the landings were going to be.

21. The traditional figure for allied death toll of D-Day had been given as 2,500. However further research puts the toll now at more than double the original figure.

22. The landings were a success but did not, on the whole achieve their ambitious objectives. The British hoped to take the City of Caen on D-Day; in fact, it was only captured after over a month of terrible fighting.

23. The fighting during the Battle of Normandy, that followed D-Day, was as bloody as it had been in the trenches of the First World War. Casualty rates were slightly higher than they were during a typical day during the Battle of the Somme in 1916.

24. The morning after D-Day the police raided a brothel, which French women had set up in a wrecked landing craft.

Part Three

World War Two

Hollywood Heroes

Hollywood War Heroes
Famous actors who served in WII

Regardless of their fame, lifestyle, and on-going movie projects, many Hollywood actors enlisted in WWII.

Not only did they contribute to the war effort, but also inspired many young men to do the same.

Many of them deserve to be honoured for risking their lives to save the American Nation.

Even though the list is long and some of the names might surprise you, here are just a few stars who served in the military, before or after showing up on the big screen.

Charles Bronson

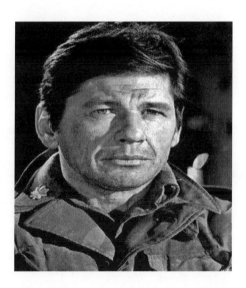

"I might never have found the outside world if I hadn't been drafted into the Army," said Charles Bronson, the legendary actor who starred as the anti-hero in Death Wish, the nemesis of Henry Fonda in Once Upon a Time in the West, and one of the members in The Magnificent Seven.

He was born Charles Buchinsky in Johnstown, Pennsylvania and raised in a very impoverished family of 15 children. He had to start working in a coal mine at the age of ten, and once he even had to wear his sister's dress to school because there literally wasn't anything else for him to wear.

When he enlisted in the U.S. Army Air Forces in 1943, Bronson found himself for the most dangerous assignment — as a tail gunner. It was the position with the highest casualty rates during the WWII.

Fortunately, Bronson survived 25 missions in the "airman's coffin" and was awarded a Purple Heart after the end of the war.

Charlton Heston

"You can take my rifle … when you pry it from my cold dead hands" were the words of Charlton Heston, the actor who played Moses in The Ten Commandments, and who won an Academy Award for Best Actor for his epic portrayal of Judah Ben-Hur in Ben Hur.

Well, his military career is also impressive. Heston joined the military in 1944 as served as a radio operator and aerial gunner on a B-25 Mitchell for two years. Later, he reached the rank of staff sergeant during WWII.

In fact, Heston was stationed in the Alaskan Aleutian Islands and never saw combat, but after becoming a celebrity, he was asked by the military to narrate some highly classified military films about nuclear weapons, designed to instruct service members and employees of the Department of Energy.

He was a Conservative, and a great supporter of Reagan and Nixon, in his later years Heston was a five-term president of the NRA.

Paul Newman

Another Academy Award winner, for his performance in The Colour of the Money, Paul Newman's passion and ambition during his youth was to become a pilot.

In 1943, he joined the Navy's V-12 program at Yale University but after discovering that he had colour blindness, Newman was sent to boot camp and qualified as a gunner and radioman.

USS Bunker Hill

During WWII, in 1945, his unit was assigned to the USS Bunker Hill which fought in the Battle of Okinawa.

However, Newman didn't make it to the aircraft carrier. In a stroke of fate, his pilot developed an ear infection, grounded the plane, and the unit was held back from flying in the Okinawa campaign.

Battle of Okinawa

USS Bunker Hill was destroyed by two kamikaze attacks in quick succession, resulting in more than 600 casualties.

After being discharged in 1946, Newman was awarded the World War II Victory Medal, American Area Campaign Medal, and the Good Conduct Medal.

James Stewart

Jimmy Stewart was already a famous movie star nominated for a few Academy Awards when he enlisted in WWII. Unlike the other actors in our list, he already had a noted military career under his belt. He was also the first American movie star to enlist in WWII and remains the highest-ranking actor in military history, reaching the rank of Brigadier – General in the US Airforce

Lt. Col. James T. Stewart & Major Clark Gable – RAF Polebrook, 1943.

Stewart came from a family with a tradition of service in the Army. Although most of them were previously in the infantry, as a passionate pilot with a flying license, Stewart took to the skies during the war.

He also participated in the Vietnam War and rose to the rank of Brigadier General in the U.S. Air Force Reserve.

Among the numerous military awards that Stewart received were two Distinguished Flying Crosses, four Air Medals, French Croix de Guerre with bronze palm, Presidential Medal of Freedom, National Defense Service Medal, and the WWII Victory Medal.

Clark Gable

Even "The King of Hollywood" Clark Gable enlisted in WWII. In January 1942 he lost his third wife, Carol Lombard, in a plane crash. Gable was devastated and came to the conclusion that the only thing that could rally his spirit was joining the Army.

So, he wrote a telegram to President Franklin D. Roosevelt asking to be enlisted so that he could contribute to the war effort.

On August 12, 1942, Gable joined the U.S. Army Air Corps as a gunner, and upon completing the 12-week training, he was commissioned as a second lieutenant and participated in numerous high-profile combat missions.

Eddie Albert

Was awarded a Bronze Star at Tarawa Beach

Band leader Alton Glenn Miller

Miller really wanted to serve his country. Because he was too old (age 38 at the time), the Navy turned down his services. The noted band leader and composer actually had to convince the Army Air Forces to accept him, by saying he wanted to lead a "modernized army band." And it worked. He and his band would go on to do a weekly radio broadcast that was so successful, he was upgraded to a special 50-piece band that travelled all over the world playing for troops. In England alone, he and his group gave 800 performances. On December 15, 1944, Major Glenn Miller was on his way to Paris when his plane disappeared. Neither Miller nor the plane have ever been found.

David Niven

Pushing aside for a moment the issue of his insubordination and resigned commission from the Argyll and Sutherland Highlanders in 1933, David was the sole British Hollywood star to come back and enlist when the war began against, it should be noted, the advice of the British Embassy. He soon joined the Commandos, leading "A" Squadron GHQ Liaison Regiment, better known as "Phantom." He was part of the invasion of Normandy after D-Day, helped to set up the BBC Allied Expeditionary Forces radio service, and on his return to Hollywood, was presented with the Legion of Merit, by President Eisenhower.

He also gave this wonderful quote about his experiences: "I will, however, tell you just one thing about the war, my first story and my last. I was asked by some American friends to search out the grave of their son near

151

Bastogne. I found it where they told me I would, but it was among 27,000 others, and I told myself that here, Niven, were 27,000 reasons why you should keep your mouth shut after the war."

British Celebrities who served in World War II

Stewart Grainger

Stewart Grainer enlisted into the Gordon Highlanders at the start of the war, but he later transferred to the Black Watch and was commissioned a second Lieutenant. But was medically discharged because of a stomach ulcer in 1942.

Jon Pertwee

The most Bond-like character in this list, Jon's role in Naval Intelligence was so covert he had to keep quiet about it for decades, but a recently-published interview in Doctor Who magazine reveals he actually worked alongside Ian Fleming, and was the perfect superspy, offering brass buttons that hid a compass, a pipe that could fire a bullet, a secret map hidden in a handkerchief, and that sort of thing.

Roald Dahl

Not just the author of Charlie and the Chocolate Factory, and Fantastic Mr. Fox, Roald was an actual flying ace in the RAF, who began the war in the cockpit of a biplane (the already out-dated Gloster Gladiator), had a horrific crash when his navigation instructions took him far away from a safe landing (and was temporarily blinded too), then flew Hawker Hurricanes in the Battle of Athens. He was taken out of active flight service in 1942, and began two careers at once after that. One in writing, retelling RAF stories and writing propaganda for the Allies, and the other in international espionage, alongside one Ian Fleming.

Alec Guinness

The future Obi Wan Kenobi was in the Royal Navy, commanding a landing craft depositing troops and supplies during the invasion of Sicily and Elba. This did not distract from his already-established acting career. He was granted special leave to go and appear on Broadway during the war: Flare Path, by Terence Rattigan, is about RAF Bomber Command. No boats required.

Patrick Moore

The British astronomer and broadcaster actually joined the RAF at the age of 16, having lied about his age. He began as a navigator in Bomber Command, and then moved up to the rank of flight lieutenant, having trained in Canada, and even met Albert Einstein in New York, while on leave.

Sadly, Patrick's war ended in tragedy, with the death of his fiancée, a London nurse called Lorna, whose ambulance had been struck by a falling German bomb. He never married, having decided that she was the only love for him.

Dirk Bogarde

A commissioned officer in the Queen's Royal Regiment, Dirk became a Captain and saw active service in Europe and in the Pacific. He claimed he had been one of the first Allied troops to reach the concentration camp at Bergen-Belsen, in April 1945, although this has since been contested by his biographer. What's clear is that he saw a lot of action, and this largely informed his views in later life; including an aversion to Germans, and strong views in support of voluntary euthanasia.

Christopher Lee

Not one to shy away from a cause, Christopher actually volunteered to fight for Finland during the Winter War of 1939, but was kept away from the field of battle, along with other British would-be soldiers. Still, he found his way into the RAF, and having trained as a pilot and found to have weak eyesight, served his time in intelligence. His became a Cipher Officer in Northern Africa, heading up through Sicily and Italy, and served as a Special Operations Executive, attached to the SAS. And even after the war, Christopher continued to serve, taking a role in tracking down Nazi war criminals, before commencing on a long and impressive film career.

Denholm Elliott

Another former member of the RAF, Denholm trained as a sergeant radio operator and gunner and serving with No. 76 Squadron RAF under the command of Leonard Cheshire. His Handley Page Halifax bomber was hit by flak during a 1942 air raid on Flensburg in Germany and had to ditch in the North Sea off the German coast. Denholm was picked up and arrested and sat the rest of the war out in a prisoner of war camp in Silesia.

Audrey Hepburn

The most startling tale of them all. A condensed version of all the facts would start with a fascist father, a broken home, a relocation to Holland at the outbreak of war, the invasion of the Germans and ballet training for the young Audrey. Then malnutrition, anæmia, respiratory problems, and œdema, followed by silent ballet recitals to raise funds for the Dutch resistance, and delivering messages and parcels for them too. Once the Germans had been ousted by the British, there was more malnutrition, starvation and then finally United Nations Relief supplies. It's no surprise she became such an ardent supporter of UNICEF in later life.

About the author

William K Mackie is a native of Aberdeen, Scotland. A Veteran of both the Royal Navy and British Army. William tried his hand at Politics and stand-up comedy, before finally becoming preacher.

William is a former Member of the British Society of Criminology, as well as being a former Member of the Centre for Crime and Justice Studies both based at Kings College, London.

He went on from there and became an Author, a Broadcaster, a Covenanter and a Missionary.

Now registered as Partially Sighted, in part due to Military service, he is a Member of the Scottish War Blinded, where he receives assistance that helps him cope with his sight loss.

William had been offered the chance of a Commission into the Royal Army Chaplains' Department as a Captain ("B" Class Commission - working with Cadets only) but had to decline due to health issues.

The author, when serving with the Gordon Highlanders
in Armagh, Northern Ireland in 1979

The Books by the same author
Currently on sale

"Denis Law - an icon of the 20th Century" was supposed to be the only book and is sold to raise funds for the Regimental Museum of the Gordon Highlanders in Aberdeen.

"Do you know who I am" - [not the original title] was not meant for publication, but then it became part of a trilogy.

"You can't hear Gods voice at 4 o'clock in the morning." The title of this book came about when I had a disagreement with my then Pastor who told me that I could not hear God speaking at 4 am, in my own house unless there was a Pastor or Elder present. When I handed him my Bible and asked him to show where I the Bible is says what he had just told me. He replied, "There you go again being all charismatic."

"The devil doesn't close down churches GOD does" is the final part of the trilogy

"Yesterday's Man" is a collection of works by the late Rev Duncan Campbell, best remembered for the Lewis Revival 1949-52.

"Serving GOD not man" is the trilogy mentioned above in one volume with added chapters.

"Conflict in the Temple GOD versus Soros" This is an in depth look at Hungarian born Jew, Gyorgy Schwartz. He changed his name to George Soros, and he now owns the American Democratic Party.

"Lead me not into Temptation, I'll find it for myself" This is an in depth look at how the Christian Church globally has watered down the message of Christ and HIS Gospel, and the morals of our society have gone so far downhill because of this that only a Global Miracle can rectify this problem.

"Where Satan's seat is...." This is part Bible Study, part History Lesson, and part WAKE UP CALL. Revelation 2:13 Authorized King James Version, "I know thy works, and where thou dwellest, even where Satan's seat is: and thou holdest fast my name, and hast not denied my faith, even in those days wherein Antipas was my faithful martyr, who was slain among you, where Satan dwelleth."

This book above, links, Revelation 2:13 with Hitler, the European Parliament, Yasser Arafat and Obama.

"Serving GOD not man." This is a compilation of my trilogy of books, now in this one volume with added material, so really it is now a trilogy in four parts.

"Does this mean that I'm too late?" - Looks at the Rapture and at who is most likely be left behind when the Rapture actually happens. "Hell is hot, time is short, Jesus is returning ready or not."

"The Wooden Horse of ISLAM" and in-depth look at the "Silent invasion of Islam" across Europe and America.

"Billy Sunday" This is the second in the series "Yesterday's Man" with a collection of his most notable sermons.

"Vernon Johns" Another in the "Yesterday's Man" series. This time focusing on the "Father of Americas Civil Rights Movement". This book is a joint project with Patrick Louis Cooney PhD, he granted me access to the work that he had collated on Dr Johns, but back in the 1990's Dr Cooney (an African American) was unable to publish his book, because at the time it was deemed to be racist.

"There were two wolves" I got the idea for this book from an old Cherokee tale. There are two wolves inside each of us. One is pure evil, and the other is everything nice. They are constantly fighting. Which wolf wins depends on which one you feed. In other words, you choose where you want to spend eternity.

"Halloween and Christianity – a warning". This is a booklet that explains why Halloween and Christianity are NOT compatible.

"LORD! Your church has lost its way" In view of how many churches of all denominations have been bowing to the pressures of "Political awareness", by watering down their sermons so that their congregations do not get upset or offended. Church leaders are praying to God to ask for a blessing to their nation. If you want your nation to be blest, go back to basics with your bible in hand and STOP Legalising SIN.

Books compiled by the same author

"Agano Jipya" The New Testament in Swahili

"Biblia Takatifu" The Complete Bible in Swahili

Books by other family members

"Granny Mackie's Austerity Handbook"

By Heather E. M. Mackie

Printed in Great Britain
by Amazon

13793119R00095